# PEW PAIN

## A SPIRITUAL MEMOIR

Rev. Alexis H. Allen B.S., M. Div
2024

Copyright © 2024 Rev. Alexis H. Allen B.S., M. Div

All rights reserved. No part of this publication may be reproduced, distributed, or transmitted in any form or by any means, including photocopying, recording, or other electronic or mechanical methods, without the prior written permission of the publisher, except in the case of brief quotations embodied in critical reviews and certain other noncommercial uses permitted by copyright law.

# Foreword

Years ago, I was a professor of History of Christianity at Hood Theological Seminary in Salisbury, North Carolina. Hood is a seminary sponsored by the African Methodist Episcopal Zion Church. It is rooted in the black church tradition but is denominationally and racially diverse. In over a decade of teaching there I had a part in helping many men and women develop their hearts, minds, and skills in various kinds of ministry spanning the gamut from congregational to institutional settings. One such student is Reverend Alexis H. Allen. She was one of my students and I also had the privilege of being her academic adviser.

We have kept in touch over the years and recently she reached out to me and asked if I would be willing to read a manuscript that she had written. I agreed to read. It is a kind of a spiritual memoir focused on sharing and reflecting on things she experienced as a church member and as a church leader. From childhood she says she was taught that "the church was a hospital..." But she continues and says, "It wasn't long before I came to know that the place of healing could also be a place of severe hurt."

She titles the book Pew Pain. It is a challenging and compelling read. Sometimes I had to put it down. But, I could not leave it. It kept drawing me back. She shares stories of difficult situations that she has experienced and witnessed.

Allen writes, "Pew Pain is not written as slander. Rather, it is written to encourage honest inventory and critique for the betterment of the greatest of God ordained institutions." In the end I asked Reverend Allen if I could write a foreword to the book to commend it to people in pews and in pulpits that know what it is like to deal with pain and suffering. Allen vividly describes pain, but she also proscribes healing wisdom that are not pat answers but rather compassionate insights.

Rev. Horace Means II, PhD

# Testimonials

**Pew Pain Journey... ...**

I would like to extend my heartfelt gratitude to this extraordinary author, preacher and chaplain. Her words have not only graced the pages of this book but have also touched the hearts and souls of countless individuals through powerful sermons and spiritual guidance.

Reverend Alexis H. Allen's gift for preaching and unwavering dedication as a chaplain have been a source of inspiration to many. It is an honor to have had the opportunity to work with her on this project. Her insight, wisdom and eloquence have enriched this book in ways that words can scarcely capture.

I would also like to express my appreciation to all of those who have supported and encouraged the author on this journey, as well as the congregations and communities that have benefited from her ministry. Her collective faith and devotion have undoubtedly played a significant role in shaping the person and writer that we acknowledge today.

Lastly, I want to thank all the readers who will embark on this literary journey. May the words penned by the author resonate with your spirit and illuminate the path to greater understanding, faith and compassion.

*Dianne Horton, M. Div, BCC*
**Manager Chaplaincy and Clinical Ministries**
**Lexington Medical Center, Lexington, NC**

## Pew Pain Experience... ...

Proverbs 18:14 NIV reads, *"A man's spirit will endure sickness, but a crushed spirit who can bear?"* Having been a lifetime church member, daughter of a music minister, leader in the church and wife of a pastor for twenty-four years, I have personally experience pew pain and heard of other pew sitters who have also. Church hurt as I like to call it, is real and can be devastating to the spirit if not addressed, appropriately handled and diminished.

I believe that most people in the church have been hurt at some point in their lives. This is a reality that we do not like to talk about. I commend Rev. Alexis H. Allen for bringing to light an array of experiences where individuals have been let down, wounded, or trust has been broken by someone in the church.

Do not leave the church. Pray, read the Word of God, confront the wrongdoing, involve a faithful, loyal friend to stand by your side, act in love and examine your life to make sure you are not guilty of hurting others.

Let's commit to keep moving forward in forgiveness.

*Vickie Miller*
**Lexington, North Carolina**

# Dedication

In loving memory of some very special people who motivated and blessed me during challenging times. I treasure your memory.

**Elder Edna Springs Coleman**: my dearest friend who became closer than a sister at a time in my life when I didn't think true and deep friendship could ever happen. We both truly knew the meaning of ***Pew Pain***.

**Rev. Calvin Runnels:** first Black Chaplain Supervisor in the Department of Chaplaincy and Pastoral Education at Wake Forest Baptist Health. My Pastor, supervisor, and friend who encouraged me and required nothing less than my best, I will be forever grateful.

**Brother Frank O'Donnel:** Marianist Brother, lawyer, and educator. A devoted Catholic with a broad perspective on life and suffering.

**Elsie M Hall**: my surrogate mother bought me an old typewriter for $5.00 using half of the rent money and encouraged me to write. I was ten years old.

# Contents

Foreword .................................................................................. iii
Testimonials ............................................................................... v
Dedication ............................................................................... vii
Introduction ............................................................................ xiii

Chapter I – Connecting the Dots.................................................... 1
Chapter II – Why We Don't Talk About It ..................................... 17
Chapter III – A Hole in My Soul................................................... 29
Chapter IV – A Reward From Him ............................................... 37
Chapter V – I Once Was Young .................................................... 43
Chapter VI – Heaven Help Us....................................................... 49
Chapter VII – Bullies Everywhere ................................................. 61
Chapter VIII – From the Pew To the Pulpit ................................... 71
Chapter IX – Congregational Care................................................. 79
Chapter X – "So, Let's Do It" ........................................................ 99

Refuge… Renewal… Redemption… .............................................. 111
After the Benediction ................................................................... 115
Acknowledgments ........................................................................ 119
About the Author ......................................................................... 123

"When nothing else could help
Love lifted me."

Howard E. Smith/James Rowe/Michael T. Smith

# Introduction

*"I was glad when they said unto me let us go into the house of the Lord."*
*(Psalm 122:1 KJV). "For where two or three gather together in my name, there I am in the midst of them."* (Matthew 18:20 KJV)

God is everywhere…everywhere, is what I was taught. I believed that God was with me when I needed Him, and God was watching when I wasn't doing what I should. However, I was taught that the greatest presence of God was in the church. I was born and raised in Baltimore, MD, and as a child, I sat and listened as they prayed and invited God in. I wondered if God heard them and if He would accept the invitation. They said the church was a hospital, so I thought that in church, you could get a giant band-aid that would fix any boo-boo. It wasn't long before I came to know that the place of healing could also be a place of severe hurt.

Many of us take our seats in the church, believing we've come to the right place to connect with God and the right people. We believe that this decision will bring us a better life. We trust that we will be well-guided, encouraged, and comforted in the church.

***Pew Pain*** is not written as slander. Rather, it is written to encourage honest inventory and critique for the betterment of the greatest of God-ordained institutions. Assessments should be made as ungodly issues are worked on. Leadership should seek reputable counsel as actions that create hotspots and social gathering places of convenience for mistreatment and wrongdoing are weeded out. Everyone must be held accountable.

I am grateful for the church and cannot imagine what my life would have been without it. Many of us love the church but must admit that it has also caused us much hurt. There is a saying: "There is no hurt like church hurt." It is important to remember that church can be a very important part of children's development. The lessons taught and learned can influence their thoughts and attitudes toward the church and its people throughout their lives.

This book was not written for the perfect people in the perfect church to point fingers. Clearly, there is no such perfection. Some churches are just better fits based on beliefs and individual needs. As though racial separatism is not enough, in the Black church, we are separated even more by denominations, beliefs, sexism, ageism, and economics. 11 o'clock on Sunday mornings is the hour of great divides.

Dr. Samuel Vauvert Dansokho, an associate professor of Religion and Society and a faculty member of Hood Theological Seminary, where I was a student. He greatly influenced and encouraged my approach to this project. In 2005, he taught a rarely offered class, Women's Voices, for a group that had only seven members, including the professor and two very curious male students. We studied selected women of the Bible, their voices, and the relevance of Biblical history to the lives of women in today's society. The professor repeatedly reminded us that, as women in ministry, it was extremely important to use our voices to address issues. Each student was encouraged to find ways to express their concerns. My greatest concern was the pain of the people in the pew and the responsibility of the organized church toward the needs of the people.

For the next three years, Dr. Dansokho and I talked about the topic and the need to be transparent. He was always enthusiastic. We engaged in hours of conversation about the book I was to write. He said he believed God had given me the voice to speak for many in the church without a voice for one reason or another. Dr. Dansokho warned me that I would be confronted by many haters of the truth and the haters of the church who are happy to point to all of the wrongs of the church. He said, "Don't let any of this stop you. In order for there to be change, there first must be controversy."

About the nay-sayers, the professor couldn't have been more right. Several people choose not to talk with me once I shared my pursuit. One friend in tears begged me to give up the idea. "We are trying to get people to come into the church. Your words will only make them not want to come." I received a warning from a male minister who believed he was telling me for my good. "You know that it is hard for women as ministers in the church. The things you want to say and put in writing will only make it harder for you and other women in ministry." Upon hearing this, I only regret that I was not fiercely fueled to go forth with full speed.

Following one of the many intense conversations with the professor, the next time I stood in the pulpit to preach, I looked out and imagined people in pews everywhere. I wondered how many of them felt like the heavy-hearted doorkeeper who opened the door time and again and welcomed the people into this particular church, a place that she knew was in silent disarray and in desperate need of repair. That Sunday, my sermon topic was *The People In the Pew*.

My understandings come from the Black Church experiences I grew up with, chose as an adult, and served in. However, we know that people are people, and no perfect churches exist. I met a lady with a friend who was a student at the same seminary I attended. We engaged in conversation about the church. She said to me, "Honey, I don't know what goes on in the Black Church, but let me tell you a little story about what happened in my White Church right here in North Carolina up near the mountains. Some people in the church didn't know any better and just thought everything was perfect." She said, "We had a young preacher, and he was as handsome as they come. I am telling you, he was a good-looking young man who could preach. We couldn't wait to get to church. Come to find out, he was writing secret love letters to half the women in the church. He had convinced each of them that he was in love with them and only them. Well, one young woman shared the secret with her best friend only to discover that her best friend had the same secret. When it all got out, and the husbands got involved, let me tell you, what a mess it was in that church," she said with a smile. We shared a girlish giggle and parted with my thinking that she, too, had received one of those secret love letters. Her smile suspected my thinking so.

We compliment and are grateful for the workers of God who accept the calling to shepherd the people of God. Guiding the lives of others can be a daunting responsibility given the situations and challenges of life we all face. However, the Word of God speaks: "And how shall they preach except they be sent? As it is written, "How beautiful are the feet of them that preach the gospel of peace and bring glad tidings of good things!" ( Romans 10:15 KJV) "... be shepherds of the flock that God gave you, and look after it willingly, as God wants you to, and not unwillingly. Do your work, not for mere pay, but for a real desire to serve." (1 Peter 5:2 Good News Bible)

From the pulpit to the door, we each have a role in helping to make the House of God the best it can become. Everyone in the church deserves respect and consideration, as everyone will be affected. *Is this the church that God is proud of?* We must ask ourselves, and then we must collectively work toward making it that church. Together, let us work toward removing scars. Our lives can be improved as we move toward healing from **Pew Pain.**

*AHA*

CHAPTER I

# Connecting the Dots

*"But where shall wisdom be found?
And where is the place of understanding"*
(Job 28:12 KJV)

I grew up as a part of everyone's church. What I remembered most about sitting in the pews of my great-grandmother's church infused and confused my thinking about church and church folk. My head seemed filled with tangled thoughts like a clear balloon filled with knotted strings. As I looked around, I wondered if everyone knew my thoughts. Maybe they could help me, or maybe they would punish me for all of my twisted thinking.

Grandma Smith was my great-grandmother and the grandmother of my mother. Her name was Drucilla Smith. She was born in 1892 and died in 1992, just a few days short of becoming a centenarian. She long outlived her husband, her one child, who was my mother's father, and one adopted daughter. Her funeral was held at the third and present location of the Gillis Memorial church in Baltimore, Maryland, where she was a faithful member. Her parents were among the organizers and founders when the church began at its first location in Stockton Street. It continues to be a well-known, active, and thriving church in the Black community.

At Grandma Smith's home-going celebration were one remaining grandchild, her great-grandchildren, great-great grandchildren, and great-great-great grandchildren. It began in the childhood presence of my great-grandmother that my little mind seemed to be all out of place in my little body.

There was my Godmother who shared raising me with my mother. She worshipped at everybody's church and took me along. Denomination was irrelevant. There was Mama Annie, my father's mother, a devoted Catholic, and Mama Hilda, my mother's mother, who divided her time between home, work, and the AME church. Like mother hens, all of these women took me under their wings, and if I had no place else, they took me to church.

There was Morning Star Baptist Church. It was just across Fayette Street and up the block from where we lived. Like so many other little children in our neighborhood, we walked to church being led by adults who went from door to door to gather us for Sunday school. There was no such thing as a church van, and we gave no thought to it. Upon arrival, our teachers always warmly welcomed us. As part of our lesson, we were given Sunday School Cards with a Biblical picture on one side and a little story on the other. My sister Loretta and I proudly kept them like trading cards. Morning Star Baptist Church was a good place for me, and it was what I believed the church and the people were supposed to be like.

When my sister and I were a little older, we visited the storefront Pentecostal churches in our neighborhood. We would quietly sneak in and find a seat in the rear corner. Unlike any of the churches the adults took us to, they praised God. We watched the shouting and dancing, listened to the loud rhythmic music and drumbeats, and shared our thoughts. On the way home, there was always much more to talk and laugh about. I couldn't have imagined the richness of these experiences.

As a child, I believed everything was like the pages in my coloring book, where you draw the lines to connect the dots. If you took time and were careful, the picture would become clear. Then, all you needed to do was add the colors. At the age of five, I did not know the word hypocrisy but recognized that too many links were in the chains of the church, and the people of the church were broken. The dots were not connecting for me, and the colors were blurry. I remember thinking and feeling that something was really wrong with me.

My daunting views began in the church of my great-grandmother. Her behavior seemed so opposite to my understanding of what was taught me in the other churches I attended. This was the beginning of gnawing issues that continue to haunt me. No matter how I tried, I could not connect the dots. It didn't make sense to me then, and I understood it even less as time passed. I thought you went to church to learn how to be good and how to be kind and nice. I thought that if you were good and didn't get your clothes dirty, everyone would be nice to you. There were so many unconnected dots.

Grandma Smith lived in an amazing 12-room plus house in the 1000 block of West Fayette Street. There was always talk that I didn't understand as to how it was afforded following the great depression. My mother's name was Delores. She was fourteen and pregnant when her mother sent her to live with her fraternal grandmother. The year was 1943.

I don't know my mother's daily chores, but she told me that on Saturday mornings, she had to start with the rooms on the third floor and scrub every room on her hands and knees until she reached the first floor.

Then she had to walk several long blocks to the market and walk back carrying two grocery shopping bags. Her grandmother thought the strenuous chores might cause her to miscarry, which would be best given the circumstances. My mother said that while on her hands and knees scrubbing, she went into labor. The baby girl was born a preemie but very much survived. My mother turned 15 when the baby turned two months old. She named her Patricia.

My parents married when my mother was 16 and my father was 18. With some help from my fraternal grandparents and other family members, they moved into a nice little house on the corners of two small streets: Carlton and Vine. It was one long block away from where Grandma Smith lived. I was born in that house, the third of my mother's nine children, when my mother was almost eighteen.

My mother's firstborn was raised by her mother, who lived in Pigtown, a neighborhood in South Baltimore. The community got its name because when the pigs were unloaded from the trains, they were run through the streets to the slaughterhouses. My mother shared that being a child mother, not knowing what to expect, and the treatment that she received at the hands of her grandmother made life very confusing and very hard.

Though she was a child in the home with her father and grandmother, my mother never said anything about her father protecting her. I remember seeing him only once. I was asleep in bed, and my mom woke me. He sat on my bed, talked gently, and gave me a teddy bear. I loved that little bear and named it Buster. I remember crying when our house caught fire, pleading for someone to save Buster.

"I don't like her. She made you cry," I said to my mother. "It's all right," my mother said. "She has made me cry many tears." The difference was, this time, I watched as it happened. I was maybe four, and my sister was a year and a half older. I had not yet started school. It was a confusing time because I wanted everyone to like me, and I think I wanted to like everyone. The person I didn't like was Grandma Smith.

Even in the worst of situations, it was important to my mother to keep everything as clean and neat as possible. If there had been a label for my mother at the time, it probably would have been OCD, obsessive-compulsive disorder. I remember tears streaming down my mother's face as she wrapped something up very carefully, neat, and tight in brown paper. We left home to walk the distance down Vine Street along the back of Grandma Smith's house. My mother held the package securely under her arm as she stepped in a deliberate kind of painful silence, firmly holding the hands of my sister Loretta and mine. We knew where we were going. Soon, we would find out why.

The tall fence surrounding Grandma Smith's house's backyard was designed to spark the imagination of the curious but to keep them out. My mother opened the gate and guided us in first. Grandma Smith and several of her friends were sitting in the metal yard chairs that always appeared freshly painted. It must have been another one of her parties as all the ladies sat in a circle holding tall glasses with something refreshing. Grandma looked at us like the uninvited guests that we were. That day, we were tolerated as outsiders. She offered us nothing.

Tears streamed down my mother's face as she walked toward the chair where her grandmother was sitting. My mother handed her the package from under her arm and said, "Grandma, how could you do this to me?

This meat has skippers in it. It's not right, Grandma. It's not right!" Grandma Smith never moved in her seat, reacted, or appeared concerned. She handed the package back to my mother and said in a voice not much louder than a whisper, "Dee, all you have to do is put it in some boiling water and the skippers will come out. Then, you can cook it." My mother took the package, dropped it on the ground near where Grandma sat, took her girls by the hands, and we left. I later learned that skippers are maggots, and I liked Grandma even less.

I will only know some of the surrounding circumstances. I know that in the early fifties, Grandma Smith appeared to live extremely well. Her large home had a summer kitchen and a well-manicured backyard with a little pond and some ducks. There was a stable and a horse. My sister told me that there was also a car and a truck later.

The years passed, and Mama had more children. Sometimes, she would send us to visit our great-grandmother. The formal dining room with the fancy lace tablecloth that draped the table always fascinated me. Everything was always so picture-book perfect. The center of the table always held a large crystal bowl filled with a fruit arrangement. The debate among us children was whether the fruit was real or artificial. Some of us said it had to be for decoration because the more we begged, the more animatedly Grandma Smith refused to give us a piece. I thought the fruit was real, and she was just plain mean to little children. I was right! One day, when we were gathered in the yard, I sneaked into the dining room, reached up on the table, got an apple out of the bowl, took a bit out of it, and put it back. Then, knowing how right I was about the fruit being real, I took a banana, squeezed it, and put it back. Now, the perfect fruit bowl was no longer perfect. Strangely, I remember feeling an odd sense of fulfillment combined with guilt. I also remember feeling anger that I could not understand. This was my secret for years. I often wondered what would have happened had I been caught. But most of all, I wondered what God thought about a bad little girl who had to know. I never had a meal at that table, nor did I remember having a happy time in my great-grandmother's house. She never hit us or raised her voice. I could have better understood that kind of meanness.

Grandma Smith boasted that her husband took really good care of her, and indeed he did. Her house sparkled with fine china, blue glassware, pretty pictures on the walls, and furniture I never saw anyone sit on. A visit to her house was like going to a museum. You just walked around and looked and listened to what seemed like a prerecorded message: "You children don't touch anything. Do you hear?" "Do you hear?" was not a question but a quiet spoken command we knew to obey. What really went on in that big house with so many rooms is open to imagination.

Grandma made and sold hot rolls that people ordered and lined up for. Other than that, she bragged that she never had to work. I remember walking to the store with my sister to get the cakes of yeast Grandma needed to make the bread. The smell of yeast bread rising and baking in the oven remains a memory. But I remembered most how we, as little children, stood around watching as the rolls came from the oven. To no avail, we begged for one. After a while, we stood wide-eyed and quiet, once again knowing that begging did not soften her heart. She always promised that when she had time, she would bake a pan of rolls and bring them to us. I understand that she did. I somehow missed the occasion.

By the time I was twelve, I was making hot rolls. They probably weren't as good as Grandma Smith's, but I don't know. I couldn't compare. I learned early that you could find anything in a book, and if you could read and follow directions, you could even make bread. My mother, sisters, and brothers liked the bread I made. When my children were growing up, I made bread often and let them joyfully eat it. For Mother's Day, my then fourteen-year-old son bought me a round glass tube with a rack to bake a loaf of bread. Many years later, my grown-up daughter bought me a bread machine as a Mother's Day gift. My children remembered the joy of freshly baked bread.

By now, the family had grown. My father disappeared to sea, so the story goes, to save himself from the mess he had created on land. My fraternal grandparents bore some responsibility for their son's behavior and assisted my mother, along with the help of my maternal grandmother. My mother met someone else and had two little boys, Gary and Gregory, who were three years old. The family kept growing to nine of us.

As a group of little children, we were Grandma Smith's "Little Darlings." When Grandma spoke to any of us, she called us "Darling." I am not sure that she knew any of our names. Several of the "Little Darlings" would walk the four or five city blocks to church, following behind Grandma Smith like little ducklings strategically obeying her lead with what I remember to be military precision. Sometimes, we would tap each other and giggle. We were careful not to let Grandma see us, though I suspect she did. Still, she looked straight ahead. Grandma Smith did not look back.

At church, the "Little Darlings" were paraded from person to person, and Grandma proudly gave a speech about how nice and clean her granddaughter kept us. One by one, we stepped forward as directed, as though we were in a commercial for laundry products. Grandma Smith seemed very proud that we were the by-products of the granddaughter she had taught and demanded cleanliness. She was a star among the church folk.

Just before the beginning of service, Grandma would strategically place us on the church bench. We knew the unspoken rules. We sat there with hands in our laps, as still and quiet as children could be. I sat beside Loretta with my tiny legs dangling from the wooden seat. I was miserable. My body was not made for the seat where I had been placed, and my mind did not seem to be made for my body. Mostly, I kept thinking that the dots did not connect. All the church people thought Grandma was so nice to the clean "Little Darlings." No one would have listened to me. I was a child, and who would believe that Grandma Smith was not the wonderful, charming church lady who showed the Love of God every minute of every day? Besides, what could anyone except God do to change her heart? I sat there in my physical and emotional pain, wondering if I even had the right to hurt or think the thoughts that I did. I felt ashamed.

Occasionally, on Friday evenings, the church held peanut scrambles. They would give the children an empty bag, and some adults would throw peanuts with the shells into the middle of the room. We would scramble to get them. It seemed fun for the others, but I was small and frail and just got pushed out of the way. They should have given us some peanuts and developed some better entertainment. I resigned to quietly sitting on the bench, uncomfortable in mind and body.

I will never know the particulars of the behaviors of my great-grandmother. Grandma Smith had a great need to display perfection in the people and things she seemed to believe in. Her anxiety may have been because the people around her were not as perfect as she wanted them to be. Her son was not perfect, her granddaughter was not perfect, and neither was her adopted daughter. My maternal grandmother told me that my grandfather was dating her and another young woman at the same time. Two days after my mother's birth, my grandfather's other girlfriend also had a baby girl. Grandma Smith had another granddaughter who was basically unacknowledged.

None of us are perfect, and certainly not the people Grandma Smith loved and tried to mold. They may have reminded her of just how imperfect she, too, was. Her only child had a son named Earl and a daughter named Delores with my grandmother and another daughter with his other girlfriend. I never heard about him marrying anyone. I heard it said that he was a "rascal." Surely Grandma Smith couldn't feel good about the church folk knowing that. Though it appeared that her life was grandeur, the reality is that the journey for each of us is like a stage play with many dark scenes behind the curtains. As a child, I could only see what was before me, the material possessions and the appearance of comfort my great-grandmother had, compared to the rest of us. Would my childhood thoughts have been different toward her if my mother had told me to like her and love her despite the tears that I watched her cause? I believe that in my mother's pain, she sought someone to join in agreement with her, and in the moment, it was me. I'm not sure what I felt. I couldn't connect the dots.

As I grew up, I made my great-grandmother invisible. I didn't know how else to handle my feelings. It also helped that I moved away from Baltimore for many years. When I returned, my sister Loretta encouraged my relationship, and I visited her occasionally. Times had changed for her as they will for all of us who live long enough. Now, she lived in a small but immaculately kept apartment that was the miniature near-perfect reproduction of the house from years past. Grandma Smith was always welcoming and still called me "Darling."

I soon learned that the disconnect between the church's teachings and how people treated one another did not begin or end with my great-grandmother. I learned that people's behavior had less to do with materialism, status, race, or money. Rather, what we hold in our hearts makes the difference.

**Ham and Oyster Dinner**

"I will never eat string beans, not ever again. All they gave us was string beans," I cried as I could not understand the good church people again. I was small for eight or nine years but always big enough to help. My birth mother and my Godmother raised me as part of the combination of all the women who helped me become who I am. I called my Godmother "Mama" and my mother "Mama." I was just blessed to have both of them. My Godmother was a woman with only a second-grade education. She had to stop school and work to help her sisters and brothers go to school. Mama always found work as a domestic and taught me that if you don't have a job, you have to make one. Because she was honest and hardworking, she was always given a recommendation. There were always odd jobs that included me. She often told employers that she could come to do the job only if she could bring her little girl. I learned work ethics early in life. This time, it was helping in the church kitchen for the Annual Ham and Oyster Dinner.

It started as an exciting adventure. The church people sent a car to pick us up. That made me feel important because Mama and I usually caught the bus wherever we had to go. It was a big church, much larger than any church in the black community where we lived. The massive white columns on the front reminded me of pictures I had seen in books. Upon arrival, we were escorted to the kitchen, where Mama immediately put on her apron and began to follow orders. I was taken to the sink, where I stood on the wooden platform made of soda crates. My job was to wash the dishes. The stainless-steel sinks seemed so big that I imagined I would fall in and drown. I envisioned myself bobbing up and down in the bubbles. The fun of it all ended just like the endless flow of dishes. I washed dish after dish and put them in the adjoining sink of hot water to be rinsed. Some church people took them out and put them in a drying rack.

There were more dishes than any little girl should have had to wash, and Mama knew it. However, she assured me that the rewards would be worth it. She said they would pay her and give us good food to take home. Inside, I was crying. I was overwhelmed with all I had to do. But I knew Mama was doing her best for us. With everything clean and only a couple of church folk left, the leftover food was wrapped and packed in cardboard boxes. They gave us one of the boxes of food and a ride home. Mama let me hold the box on my lap. I couldn't wait to have some good food, like what I saw Mama putting on plates for the people who ate in the church dining room. My little mouth watered for ham, oysters, and potato salad.

Everyone at the church that day except Mama and me was White. I didn't think that it mattered. However, I later came to believe that it did. I don't know how much money they paid Mama, but I think she gave me a dollar or two. What I remember most is that when we got to our kitchen table and opened our box of good food, the only thing it contained was leftover string beans. There were no oysters, slices of ham, and potato salad. There was no food to arrange nicely on a plate, only string beans. I cried! "I will not eat string beans. I will not eat string beans." Mama found some food for us and warmed it up with some string beans. I did not eat the string beans, and Mama did not make me.

Later in life, I thought back to that Saturday night. I hoped that I wasn't being an ungrateful brat. I knew that times were hard, and Mama was doing her best with what she had. It did not occur to me as a child that my Mama was as hurt and as disappointed as I was. Her watching my pain did not help. I sat in church the following Sunday morning, thinking about how wrong church people could be. The truth of the matter is they did not have to do anything except pay Mama. But the humane and decent thing would have been to give a mother and child something to eat other than string beans, at least a little something like the food they packed in the other boxes.

**The Poor Box**

My sister Loretta is still a devoted member of the Roman Catholic Church. We made our First Communions and Confirmations at St. Pius Roman Catholic Church, the church of Mamma Annie, our fraternal grandmother. It was located on the corner of Schroder Street and Edmondson Avenue in Baltimore, Maryland. We studied Catholicism and found the formalities and rituals interesting. Mama Annie was proud to watch her granddaughters make their First Communions and be confirmed.

The church was sacred, and the heavy, large, squeaky doors were always open. My sister and I often visited when no services were being held. It was an engaging, safe place. We were taught that God hears your prayers but that the ear of God is even better when you pray in church. And we believed this. One Saturday afternoon, we went to the Catholic Church to pray. Inside, it was dark except for the flicker from the lights of the little candles. We prayed for the money to buy our younger sister and brothers a loaf of bread. We went to the altar, put a dime in the candle box, and lit a candle. As we kneeled, we heard a sound in the rear of the church. We glanced to see one of the priests in the shadows. I still remember his name. We looked at each other excitedly and believed it was the answer to our prayers. We quietly, in haste, rushed up the aisle to approach him. We told him we had come to pray for some money so our mother could buy bread. "Can you help us please?" He said, "No, I cannot help you. Whatever you used to light the candle, you could have bought bread. Maybe you will think about it next time." Thinking he would have a change of heart, I begged, "Please, please give us .27 cents from the poor box so that we can get bread." He responded, "The money in the poor box is for the poor." He turned and walked away and went through a door out of our sight. We felt ashamed, painfully, and harshly scolded. Maybe he was right. A loaf of bread costs .27 cents, and we would have been .10 cents closer had we not lit the candle. However, we believed we were poor and had done the right things at that moment. And though, as children, we never had a lot, my sister and I always put a nickel in the poor box whenever we could.

I was heartbroken and disappointed in the man of God. Again, I was disheartened by the actions and behaviors of church folk. The priest wasn't just church folk. He was a leader, and everything I knew at the time told me that the Catholic Church was rich. Twenty-seven cents seemed like such a small request. Once again, the dots did not connect. It took me a while to understand that there are church folk and Christians.

As years passed, I felt guilty about my feelings as a small child. Why couldn't I just run and play with childlike thoughts as the other children seemed to do? After all, it could have been so much worse. I thought something was wrong with me to see things as I did. It took a while to understand that sometimes we see injustices, ignore them, and then begin to accept them as the norm. Just maybe these were the blows and surges that I needed to recognize my responsibility to help others who sat painfully in one position or another, on one kind of bench or another, almost knowing what to say and fearfully wondering if anyone would listen if they had the words.

I remember sitting Sunday after Sunday on the church bench with neatly combed and pressed hair with large bows and a face freshly polished with olive oil. My little legs dangled under the stiffly starched dresses, and I dared not squirm though such stillness seemed impossible. I knew what church behavior was. However, no one could stop the wiggling thoughts in my head about all I had yet to understand about the church and the people of God. Way back then, it was only at the beginning of many Sundays that I sat in Pew Pain.

We sit as newcomers to the church, often unable to connect the dots if we can identify them. Others have lined the benches for years, and the dots have become so blurred that they just stop trying. The assembled believers gather under the same roof to worship and read from the same book, the Bible and seem to interpret it all so differently. Some stop coming. Others stop trying and seek consolation elsewhere or in other things. For some, all is well.

> *"Understanding others is not always easy.*
> *When someone does that, they will always be misunderstood."*
> Jeevana Gogula

CHAPTER II

# Why We Don't Talk About It

*"For nothing is hidden that will not be disclosed, nor is anything secret that will not become known and come to light."* (Luke 8:17 NRSV)

We need change in the church. Admittedly, conversations about the need for change in the church are uncomfortable. However, our churches will not change if we believe this is as good as it gets. Too many believe that questioning or speaking out about church or church leadership and how we can improve the institution is speaking out against God. Quite the contrary. Our silence and do-nothingness are part of the problem. Change starts in our minds and our hearts. We take no steps to make a positive difference when we find comfort in our complacency. It is easy to become emotionally and physically effortless. Change will only come when we believe that God is expecting our best and that we are capable of giving it. "Not everything that is faced can be changed. But nothing can be changed unless it is faced." (unknown)

"Some of us just aren't strong like you, Rev. Allen. I thank God for you. Somebody needs to tell the truth for the rest of us who just aren't strong. There are so many things that they know are just not right, so many things, but what can we do? We take what we get. Let God lead you, Rev. Allen. Let Him lead you."

These were the words of one of the faithful senior members who asked to speak with me. Obliging was a pleasure. I couldn't imagine anyone turning down a request from this soft-spoken doorkeeper who was special to me from our first meeting six years prior. She told me she missed my presence at church the previous Sunday and just wanted to know why I wasn't there. I felt comfortable sharing the reason for my absence with her. "I was out of town working on a project I started several years ago," I said. "It is about the many things in the church that trouble me deeply. It was an opportunity and a blessing to work with my project mentor, who encourages me and provides professional guidance."

I don't know what, if anything, I expected her to say. However, her timely words of wisdom confirmed my path and encouraged me. God will send us unexpected messages through unexpected sources. The only outward expressions of emotions I ever witnessed from her were soft-spoken words and gentle smiles. What saddened me most were these words, "We take what we get," along with her expressing belief that in the church, other than praying, there is nothing we can do about it. I felt a new surge of energy to move forward, believing it was my assignment to put some truths held in my mind and my heart into words on paper, hoping that readers would take the lead in seeking ways to help those suffering from Pew Pain. Some of us have to be voices for the voiceless. I believe that sweet, soft-spoken doorkeeper is now helping open the doors of heaven and welcoming everyone. I believe God's message to her is "*Well done.*"

The church is said to be likened to a hospital, where people come with their sickness and pains of life with expectations of healing. The rows of pews are like benches lined up in emergency waiting rooms. Some of the patients have minor injuries, while others should be rushed to critical care. We don't talk about the church because it is shameful that so many of us have been brutally hurt in the very places where we gather with hope for help and healing. Bad situations often get worse. The wounded meet us at the door and sit among us in the pews. "Hurt people hurt people." is such a true statement. So many other things go on in the church that the real purpose seems often forgotten. Healing for the hurting may not even make the priority list. Far too many people find comfort in the pain that has become all they know.

In a recent conversation with a long-time devoted minister, with a sad expression, she said, "Things have gotten so bad in the church. There is so much darkness." I responded, "Rev., things didn't just begin to get bad. They have been that way for a long time. Some of us don't want to face harsh realities and truths and talk about it." Her response was, "You're right."

We don't want to talk about our selective blindness, deafness, and muteness as we sit in the church among those who intentionally and unknowingly harm others. Some negative behaviors have continued for as long as there have been church folk. Without thought, many bad actions have become just the way they are.

On Saturday nights, there were recreational lynchings of innocent men. Many of those who took part in entertaining murders were Sunday morning worshipers. They sat in the House of God, filled with hatred and perceived senses of superiority and power. To share the pew as the powerless wife, child, family member, or friend of those whom we know have extreme disregard for humanity will shame us.

Some children are victims of incest, abuse, and physical and emotional wounds that seem never to heal. Some mothers turn their heads in pain and shame as they pretend not to know what their husbands, brothers, boyfriends, and other relatives are doing to their children. Too many ministers and church leaders are responsible for destroying the innocence of too many children. The harm to one child is one too many. The sirens should blast, the lights flash, and there should be rounds of applause as pedophiles, men, and women, hiding behind collars and Sunday best, are taken from the church and stopped from doing more harm. The pews are lined with children in pain.

There are seniors whose family members are abusing. Some of them come to church as their only place of refuge. Many of them have outlived most of their friends and family members of their generation. As victims of elder abuse, they often sacrifice their limited incomes and meager comforts in hopes of some time and attention from their children, grandchildren, and church members. Too often, the investments have questionable returns.

Everyone comes to church on Sunday as though all is well, and the dastardly acts go unaddressed at the painful expense of those being abused. Being forced into such gross wrongs in fear and silence is excruciating. Despite the levels of disarray and failure, the church remains the safest haven many of us have.

Many Christians are ashamed of the institution that has been designed to be the most excellent in the care, nurturing, and spiritual development of its people. We are ashamed of the behaviors of our fellow Christians and ashamed of ourselves for our participation or lack of apparent ability to help make known wrongs closer to the right. The people are the church and not the building in which we assemble. We ought to be ashamed because our behaviors are often grossly contradictory to what we teach as the purpose of the assembly. In shame, we turn our heads and adjust our selective blindfolds.

"If I didn't belong to this church, I wouldn't join it," says one man about his church as he felt trapped. He had the guts to say what many others felt but was too embarrassed. I recently talked with a friend who joined his church at eight. Seventy-three years later, he moved on to another church. He knew there were problems at the church where he had spent a lifetime and worked tirelessly toward solutions, often neglecting personal matters. He gave generously, worked in the community, raised money, and worked on several boards. He shared that he stayed at that church and worked so hard because he was proud of how the church reached out to him as a child. He felt the need to do the same for other children. As new ministers were assigned to the congregation, they became less concerned with outreach and the community. Increasingly, their energies and concerns seemed to be for personal gain. Finally, he realized that he, too, was caught by the adhesiveness that keeps so many from moving on. Before it was too late, he knew he had to go. He left his church and joined one with strong outreach programs. He said that whatever time God continued to give him to serve, he had to do it in the spirit of truth. He is now 90 years old and still working in the church.

My sister Patricia told me many years ago, "The army of the Lord is the only one that kills its own troops." Spiritual maiming and murdering happen in the church. My sister deeply embraced the denomination that she grew up in. She was a dedicated member of the AME church for 65 years and served as a minister of the Gospel for 31 years. Though she told us that she was leaving due to politics and monetary demands that benefited a few at the top, it was hardly believable until the phone call came when she said, "I've given my letter of resignation and turned in my ministers license." This is not an indictment against any denomination but rather a respect for my sister, who chooses to be true to herself with whatever time she has left to serve.

For reasons none of which are good, leaders permit negative behaviors that affect many in the church. Some people can do whatever they want because their family set the cornerstone. Others buy their negative church behaviors with tithes, offerings, and checkbooks. There is the group with the ear of the pastor and pastors who sadly allow themselves to listen and buy into foolishness for the paychecks, gifts, fringe benefits, and one celebration after another that pads pockets and bank accounts. Let us not leave out the competition between the sororities and fraternities allowed to go on as though churches were houses on Greek Row.

We don't talk about it because we don't want the world on the outside to know that we distanced ourselves from the pain of one world for the pain and disappointment of another. All of this is in the church, where the captives come to be set free but all too often find themselves imprisoned in yet another kind of bondage. People on the outside know, and the sad but too often true gossip about the church is shameful. Bad experiences in the church have been why many people have left, never returned, and choose not to attend church. It doesn't make them bad or ungodly people. We handle our hurts and care for our wounds differently. I've met many unchurched people who care for others and demonstrate sincere love and concern for humanity. They set examples for those inside the walls we call the church, but they choose to stay out.

To talk about the ungodly and wrong truths of the church means that we must painfully examine ourselves in the scheme of it all. In one way or another, we are all participants in our do-nothingness, feelings of hopelessness and helplessness, lack of faith, and belief that things can change. We allow ourselves to become victims and develop the victim mentality that lulls us into the false sense of believing that it is not our fault, that we are not responsible and should not be held accountable. I have had conversations with good people and longtime members of the same congregation who told me that while my contributions and ideas were good, they were useless. "These people will never change," a longtime member said. Sadly, I recently heard the same thing from a new pastor. We have to pray for the mindsets of our present and future church leaders and those who have barely given up before they begin.

We tell people to come as they are and only accept them if they are what we think they should be. With elitist attitudes, we want people to join our ranks but then want little more from them than to be warm bodies in the seats of those who stopped by and stayed briefly once they discovered that we were not the people of God that we pretended to be. People are often ignored until the plate is passed for their contributions.

How is it that we are honoring a God we have been taught is strong and mighty, a God who has created us to carry out the plans of His will on earth? We have trouble facing the realities of what is occurring in the very places where we gather to be taught how to be disciples. Christianity is not a spectator sport. It is about more than being chained to a seat on the sidelines with invisible duct-taped mouths. It is more than being quieted with a piece of fried chicken, a scoop of potato salad, and a piece of sweet potato pie served in the church basement.

The proclaiming of Christianity is the professing of believing and following the teachings of Jesus Christ. We should not accept the "whatever" principle in the church, while some members believe that they have the right to do whatever, to whomever, whenever without respect or regard for the House of God and for all of His people. There are people who admit that they do not handle conflict well and buy into the belief that the best choice for them is to sit in Pew Pain.

We sit in the church and pew after pew, knowingly accepting being victimized by those who hold leadership positions. One example is the Pastor, who decided that he understood the problems of the wife of the couple he was counseling and chose to personally console and bed her at the expense of breaking up his marriage and her marriage and causing severe discord in the church. What about accountability for his acts, something more than "He's just a man." In ministry, women must also be held accountable for behaviors that do not represent godliness or their positions.

Many church leaders use their positions to oppress their congregations and supporters further. The gouging of financially suffering people for money so the pastor can live a life filled with luxuries should be stopped. With little or no conscience, many shepherds have fleeced their flocks. Some preachers show up to entertain and collect checks with no concern for heaven on earth or any place. We are reminded in the Gospel of Matthew 10:6 that there is to be a demonstration of the Kingdom of God here on earth. Ministers with egos bigger than life and self-serving attitudes help to create devil deacons and trustees who cannot be trusted. Leadership appointments are all too often made based on potential monetary contributions and how the pastor can be made to look bigger and better. Some leaders never show up to Bible Study or Sunday School. There is more than one down-and-dirty deacon who has fathered the child of a young girl in church. Every late-night visit has not been in the name of the Lord.

Some deacons are demons of domestic violence and mates who live in physical and emotional turmoil. Some women don't talk about it because it may ruin the reputation of the deacon in the church. Whatever the value, many women help promote the hypocrisy. Some pastors know about abuse and bad behaviors of men in the church, but rather than being objective and counseling them, they overlook it as they are all members of the same boys club. So, the lie that all is well continues. Cues are taken from ministers and leaders who set poor examples.

The former wife of an abusive pastor shared with me that her husband often struck her following Sunday morning services, especially when he was frustrated with the way things went in church that morning. Then he demanded that she redo her makeup, show up and take her seat on the front pew, and smile for the afternoon service. He was always mindful never to bruise her face, and she wore clothing that left little uncovered. She was to smile and pretend that being the pastor's wife was the best thing that ever happened in her life. How could he counsel others about abusive behaviors, given the shoes in which he walked?

There are trustees who can't be trusted with the money or anything else for that matter. Too many officers of the church lack character and integrity. There is "stealing in the name of the Lord" as an old song put it. We choose selective blindness. Rather, it is as though mistreatment is spewed through the church as if the people are either too passive or too dimwitted to do what it takes to make a difference. One associate pastor of a large affluent congregation told me that there is little to say about what happens in the church because it all could be worse. Yes, it could be. But, shame on those of us in ministry who so loosely entertain this attitude.

We don't talk about it because if and when we do, others will watch us more closely, expect us to follow Godly rules and assume greater responsibility. We may be unhappy with what surrounds us in the church, but working for change and good is real work that requires the intensity that too many are unwilling to put forth. We don't talk about it because we have resigned ourselves to accepting it as it is. We don't talk about it because it is easier to take the let God fix it approach when God has given us what we need to fix it. It's like waiting for God to come down from Heaven and flip the switch in a darkened situation when He has already provided a light switch, the electricity, and the resources to pay the bill.

When we gather in the church to align our lives with the Word of God and the saving of souls, we believe that we have put matters of guidance in the heads, hands, and hearts of Godly-led, inspired, and responsible ministers. We should be able to enter without apprehensions. Despite negative and ungodly behaviors, many leaders are placed on high pedestals; we refuse to take them down. We don't talk about our disappointment with leadership as we continue to pay them well to keep them. Men and women of God should be held to the highest standards. Bad behavior is often dismissed with, "Everybody makes mistakes."

There is fear of the unknown that we allow to hold us hostage. I've heard more than one person say, "If I leave this church, it is probably just as bad or worse someplace else." The truth is we don't know that. We stay in bad relationships, jobs that do not tap into our potential, and churches that we know are not the best for us. Sadly, we find security in our suffering. So, too many of us choose to sit in *Pew Pain*.

Our churches will not change or begin to meet God's intentions as long as we believe that this is as good as it gets and continue to be helpless contributors. Too many of us believe that to speak out against what church leaders do or fail to do is speaking out against God. Contrary to thought, our silence and nothingness are part of the problem. Taking a stand in a Godly manner does not disrespect God or leadership. Let us not find comfort in complacency. Change will come only when we believe that we deserve the best and that we are capable of helping to make it happen. "Turtles only make progress when they stick their necks out." Should we continue to refuse to discuss the insanity of the church, the insanity of the church continues!

> *"Our lives begin to end when we become silent about the things that matter"*
> Martin Luther King

CHAPTER III

# A Hole in My Soul

Congregations In Pain

*"I consider that the suffering of this present time are not worth comparing with the glory that is to be revealed to us"* (Romans 8:18 ESV)

It was 2006, and I was a Chaplin Intern at Wake Forest Baptist Hospital in Winston Salem, North Carolina. Group sessions for interns were always scheduled for Monday afternoons. Following a weekend filled with patient tragedies and bereavement, several of us eagerly awaited to hear from our supervisor. I recall interacting with a medical staff that remained professional though they were often exhausted and worn from having emptied themselves to care for others. There were emergencies and situations this past weekend that, in my mind, could have made sense to only God. The eight of us sat patiently waiting for what we believed we needed to mend our own weariness. The involvement in the depth of this level of pain and suffering in the lives of others was new to most of us. During these sessions, we listened to each other, shared cases, sometimes cried, and anxiously waited, expecting those we believed to be seasoned professionals to provide help and guidance as we attempted to unravel our emotional entanglements.

In his usual, easy-going, quiet manner, the professor and Chaplain Supervisor entered the room. For nearly the year that I'd been in his presence, the tone of his voice never changed and his mannerisms were predictably the same. In private counseling sessions, in groups, and in crisis situations, whatever the storm, he demonstrated calmness and spoke with a gentle tone of assurance, confidence, and reason. Surely it must have been his personality combined with many years of professionalism. Maybe by this time, he had just about seen it all.

The professor was always well groomed as one would expect given his position. He dressed like a meticulous Ivy League college student though those days were somewhere far behind him. Today his appearance was no exception. He was wearing his usual coordinating pullover sweater and a sports coat. His tall, well-built frame helped me imagine him on the court playing basketball in his time.

He took a seat in the circle of chairs. He sat to my right and crossed his right leg, placing it above his left knee, forming a triangle, and displaying his argyle socks. His polished tan oxfords matched the rest of his attire. But what caught my eye that day was the hole in the sole of his shoe that was about the size of a fifty-cent piece. It seemingly went unnoticed by him. In our next private session, though reluctant, I mentioned the hole in the sole of his shoe. Our session continued with an emotional conversation about the hole in the souls of all of us. Though the tops appeared perfect and polished, I never saw those shoes again. My guess is that they were somewhere in the back of a closet with the intention to one day be repaired.

Like many of us, our hidden underside is in desperate need of mending. We concentrate on the parts others easily see and often try to blind our sights to the rest. What once may have been fixed with a stitch or a Band-Aid, with the passing of time, requires major surgery. God sees it all: tops, bottoms, tarnished insides, and polished exteriors. Like the hole in the sole of the shoe that the professor seemed unaware of, invisible gaping punctures can consume the very core of our being.

In congregations everywhere, we sit among one another, hungry, thirsty, estranged, naked, sick, and imprisoned. We line the pews fragmented, seeking fulfillment, wanting to belong, to be covered, to be made well, and to be free of the binding captives that seem to cripple and confine us. Guilt, shame, and the inability to forgive ourselves and the words and actions of others hold us hostage in dark places. Tears and tatters often place us in churches among the people of God as we seek to mend. The holes may start out like those made by moths. Without repair, little hurts grow into deep valleys that swallow our spirits. Each of us is in need of repair time and again. The pains of the people are as many and diverse as there are people and the pews in which they sit.

It is impossible to know or speak about the details of individual pain. There are the obvious and visible hurts of loss that lead the list. The evident signs of aging demonstrate the loss of youthfulness and the pain of losing our physical abilities. The deaths of those we love, the loss of health, jobs, possessions, and being loved and appreciated, all cause us grief. We sometimes lose what we have worked hard to gain, including our good names and reputations. Too many children have been robbed of their innocence, a loss never to be regained. In grief and pain, our beliefs and faith are tested. Sometimes, we wonder if we will ever be alright and, if so, when. In subtlety and unseen by most, we wear the mask that hides our depression, anxiety, and emotions. We find ourselves functioning like marionettes, one string or another pulling our parts, often grateful to get by.

None of us escape hurt, humiliation, anxiety, disappointment, confusion, illness, pain, and, in the earthly end, death. Even those who appear to have been blessed with it all meet with the anxieties and pressures of life. Decisions made for selfish gain can, in turn, hurt others. It doesn't matter how good we have been, how hard we have worked, how much we have sacrificed, or how many prayers we pray; there comes a time in life when we all face challenges that seem to be insurmountable. We all face anxieties that good looks, money, fame, education, or luck do not prevent. The intensity of our pain can make us feel that our very inner beings have been ravished and invaded by forces of epic proportions. The situations of life can create holes like painful cavities that need profound fillings.

Some ministers in pulpits continue to question their purpose, their positions, and the will of God for their lives. From their places of leadership, there are many spiritual leaders who have lost touch with the reasons God called them. They face harsh realities as they look out into the faces of waiting congregants with problems and pains that mirror their own. Some Pastors cry every day because they want out of ministry but are not prepared to do anything else. Sadly, all too often, they stay, doing more harm than good to the very people who believe in them and depend on them for spiritual guidance. Wearing deceptive masks, they collect their paychecks and do little more than show up. Congregations suffer. Some children live a lifetime, never publicly acknowledged by their fathers who pastor congregations and pastors who have families on both sides of town. Some mothers continue to protect these pastors, acting as though the children were conceived through artificial insemination or unknown sperm donors.

Many Pastors are great role models and parents who, aside from all of their many obligations, take and make time for their families. There are others who miss the parenting mark. There are children of Pastors and church leaders who sit in congregations in pain, being and feeling neglected by parents who they believe love the church more than them. There are PKs (preachers' kids) who find themselves in trouble as a cry for much-needed attention.

Some people have dedicated most of their lives to the activities of their church. Yet, within the church, they are looked over, picked over, passed over, and intentionally skipped over. They line the pews feeling years of disappointment. There are many injustices among denominational leaders and ministers. Ministers are often chosen based on who raises the most money in their denominational groups as opposed to who has the heart for ministry and saving souls.

New people show up, bringing with them baggage filled with addictions, affections, and the challenges and struggles of everyday life. With nowhere else to go and nothing left to try, church may be a last resort. Yet, the territorial church folk often take too long to decide whether or not they are willing to move their baggage, some of which they've had for a lifetime. Too often, the newcomers are not given the space to unpack and start a healing process.

Church is not always the welcoming or inviting place it is advertised to be. People come seeking acceptance and too often leave because of rejection. The revolving door of the church spins once again, and while there are committees for every other reason, where is the committee that seeks to find out why people leave because staying is too uncomfortable?

While in my position as Congregational Care Pastor, I spoke with a trustee about membership, "We must do something to welcome and encourage our new members. We have an obligation to do what is necessary to help them find what they need here," I said. Then I told him about a study that I read that said that eight out of ten people who join a church leave within a year. He laughed and said, "That had to be some other church. They leave here before six months are up." I was bothered that the seriousness of the matter was taken so lightly. Interestingly enough, it is always the fault of the newcomers that they don't stay, according to some ministers and the longtime members who seem to have difficulty examining themselves.

The objectives tend to differ from one congregation to another. I know of one large and established church where the word "club" is descriptively placed in front of the church name. The members seem to be proud of the association with their reputation. While this particular church is one with exceptional musical talent and lively worship, the issue is perception. People sit in pews feeling unaccepted by the other club members. I question the requirements for membership as well as congregational objectives. An un-churched friend once shared with me that while attending a political meeting, she was in conversation with a lady who invited her to church. The invitation is said to have gone something like this. "Oh, you should consider joining my church. We have people with doctorate degrees and many other professionals. We have educated people at my church." The listener was a high school graduate who, in my opinion, has done very well with her life. She was offended by the conversation and knew that she would not be welcomed at that church. She had maintained a job for more than thirty years, which provided her with a comfortable life and retirement. Though she never attended college, she was proud that she had helped several of her family members to achieve their college goals. The truth is, I know that at that church, and like many other churches, there is a class conflict between those who believe they have arrived, members with turned-up noses, and the others who are looked down on. What happened to inviting people to the House of God because we care about their spiritual, emotional and physical well-being? Yes, there is the saying, "Birds of a feather flock together." and the flocks and groups in the church are not always welcoming to new birds.

There are some churches where the atmosphere is friendly and welcoming. If we survive the initiation, we may find ourselves in a good place that is a good fit, a place where there is the support to help us move from where we are to where God would have us to go and develop into what He would have us to be in life.

For about three years, I was a member of a small church in a small town called Midway, NC. Everyone was polite, and the people were very friendly during my first visit. After some time, one of the members shared with me that they were waiting to see if I would be comfortable with them. At the time there were only two or three other college graduates who attended. While the congregation helped many of its young people to attend college, once they graduated, they moved on, usually to places that had greater opportunities. These, however, were the people who taught me the real meaning of having a church family. They looked out for each other, and they looked out for me. I had the opportunity to be in kinship-like relationships that were greater than those I shared with many in my biological family. I continue to stay in contact with the members of that congregation and recall how the experience truly blessed me.

We seek safe places to belong, to be loved, accepted, and protected. We expect that the church is where we can work on our life issues without risk and judgment by others who also have life issues. Let the church be the place to experience the *"foretaste of glory divine"* that we sing about.

*"There is no coming to consciousness without pain,"* Carl Jung, an influential psychiatrist and founder of analytical psychology.

CHAPTER IV

# A Reward From Him

*"But the mercy of the Lord is from everlasting to everlasting upon them that fear him, and his righteousness unto children's children;"*
(Psalm 103:17 KJV)

"Children don't have problems." That's what they said when I was a child. My earliest memories of painful situations told me that this was far from the truth then. Now it is even further from the truth. Maybe in my childhood era, adults wanted to believe that it was easy for children if they had basic provisions: food, shelter, and clothing. I want to believe that most parents do the very best they can with what they have. When we know better, we are responsible to do better. That includes those of us in the church. We have an opportunity to help sow into the lives and development of our children and help to make meaningful impacts, given our understanding of the many complexities that so many children face daily. Helping our children doesn't require a degree in psychology. Sincere concern and the heart for a group of the most venerable among us is what is needed.

Life for our children greatly meets with challenges unlike any other time. We live in a society that all too often exhibits a lack of kindness and empathy. Many children are forced to assume responsibilities for themselves at levels at which they are not prepared. We must embrace our children with understanding and patience even when we meet with the complexities of generational differences. It has been repeatedly said and written that "Children have small voices in a very big world." Therefore, we must use our voices and resources on their behalf to help them to become their best. How we treat our children is a demonstration of the love of God and insurance to promote the continued growth of the church.

Many of our children are haunted by adult size problems for which they do not know how to seek or find solutions. "According to the Centers for Disease Control and Prevention, suicide is the third leading cause of death in young people between the ages of 10 and 24, resulting in about 4,600 lives lost in the U.S. each year. Cases have been documented in kids as young as 5 years old." (CBS News Article By Ashley Welch Nov 21, 2017)

Real Christians have a responsibility to demonstrate godlessness to help shape the social, physical, and spiritual development of our children as well as other children of God who may be new to the church and Christianity. We must think about how our treatment of children in the church plays into their thoughts as they evolve into adult worshipers. Adults either inspire or dishearten children to attend or participate in church. Times have changed. Many adults and parents do not attend church and leave the decision to their children. How we treat them and the examples we set will help shape their decisions and desires to be a part of a Christian community.

"I don't want to get old. I don't want to get old. Old people are mean." I remember crying as a child, believing that being mean was some kind of old-age sickness. Then I learned that some mean old people were mean young people. Some of our church seniors must be reminded that they, too, were once little imperfect children in need of acceptance and guidance. Being mean because you believe that you've lived long enough to bully a child is not acceptable. We all must be mindful that children are the future leaders of the church. There are church doors that have closed permanently because the congregations were composed of all senior members who have become homebound, are in care facilities, or have died. The church must have continuous growth of young people to sustain it, help it to grow, and keep it alive. If we want our children to participate freely in church, as adults, we have a responsibility to demonstrate Godliness as they grow and witness our behaviors.

With loving kindness, we must also be intentional in providing Christian Education to the children God places in our care in the church and outside of the church. Many children are faced with low self-esteem, peer pressure, and only God knows what else. They need love and attention. Coping with such issues can be devastating for those of us who have matured. Our responsibility is to help prepare our children through Biblical teachings of the historical Word of God as well as how to apply it as best they can to the reality of their young lives.

There are many programs designed to serve our children in the church. They can be tweaked based on individual group needs, levels of learning, and instructors' skills. Unlimited amounts of children's materials are available. Without excuses, children can receive Godly care, Christian education, concern, nurturing, and love through the church.

Many children sit among us in pain. A young man who grew up in foster care and in the church shared with me his thoughts. He said that all of the children in the home where he lived were frightened, and they all bore the physical and mental scars of abuse. It was evident that only minimal amounts of the monies received for the care of the children were spent on them. The children welcomed the kindness shown to them by the church folk on Sunday but asked the question "Why didn't the church folk do something to help us?" Maybe they did. They may have prayed and believed that prayer was the extent of their obligation.

How can abused and neglected children sing, *"Yes Jesus Loves Me"?* Children, as well as many adults, find it hard to understand and feel love when they are intentionally being inflicted with pain. Even in the church, people avoid becoming involved. The question should be, "What is my business?" Our answers will move us toward seeking solutions.

We are obligated to protect our children and to keep them safe, especially when they are in our care. Time and again, there are news stories of inexcusable child predators and sexual abuse scandals in the church. Children from all races, socioeconomic backgrounds, genders, and denominations are harmed by vultures like most of the abusers in the church who hide in plain sight. They hide behind the robes of evil and words from the Bible. Trust is presumed because the institution of the church is supposed to be a safe place.

Clearly, there are laws written for everyone's protection. Too often, it appears that there is more concern for the adults who harm our children than the children who have been inflicted with irreversible injuries that will follow them into adulthood and life. Great measures continue to be taken to conceal the true reputations of those who harm children in the church. We must stop looking the other way and choosing to be selectively blind! We must speak up and demand greater transparency of all in ministry who harm our children. How long must we suspect and see harmful acts being done to our children, who are innocent and defenseless, before we say something and do something about it? In wrongful silence, too many of us are complicit.

In 1996, the United Methodist Church set in place a plan to help protect children, youth, vulnerable adults, teachers, and leaders. It is entitled *Safe Sanctuary Policy*. Each individual church has a set of policies. The policies are said to be consistent with the gospel. Information about these policies and resources can be found through Discipleship Ministries of The United Methodist Church. This site provides sample policies that can be adopted for all sizes of churches and denominations. The sound comprehensiveness of these policies and available guidelines should demand the attention of those in leadership roles who are responsible for the well-being of our children as well as others in need of protection.

Church should be a safe and welcoming place in the minds of children. They should eagerly come without fear of being harmed or mistreated in any way. All children should be met with respect as church doors open wide and welcoming. They should feel accepted for who they are and welcomed as a part of the congregation. Children need patience, discipline, direction, and correction. Adults, as children of God need the same. We should not expect our children be perfect. "In youth we learn. In age we understand." (Marie von Ebner-Eschenbach) As adults we must be patient and understanding, knowing that we once were young.

Most recently, I had an opportunity to attend the closing of an ecumenical one-week arts camp for children sponsored by St. John's Lutheran Church in Salsbury, North Carolina. There was no cost to the approximately sixty children who were given wonderful opportunities to enjoy crafts and music. The children ranged in grades from rising kindergarteners to fifth grade. The participating denominations were Lutheran, Presbyterian, Catholic, Baptist, United Methodist, and Episcopal. This camp was a great example of how so many adults with different religious beliefs came together to show the love of God and help to make wonderful memories for the children. The children made beautiful little flowers and butterflies with coffee filters and marvelous sounds of music with their voices, bells, and small instruments.

The adults shared their educational professions and gifts, giving some children exposure and opportunities they may not otherwise have had. Most of all, they had hearts for the children who were far from being concerned about the theology, culture, or race of any of them. They unified to create a successful experience and positive memories. Denominational territorialism did not have a place. I believe the positive impact was beyond measure.

Childhood experiences and subconscious lessons taught by those who claim to be Christians can influence a child's relationship with the church, their feelings about worship and their questions about the love of God. As adults in the church, it is important to be mindful of the examples that we set. "Train up a child in the way he should go..." (Proverbs 22:6) We must be mindful of how we treat our children and the behaviors that we example as a part of that training. We must help our children to become their best.

*"Who plants a seed beneath the sod and waits to see believes in God"* ~ Doug Larson

## CHAPTER V

# I Once Was Young

*"And now, in my old age, don't set me aside. Don't forsake me now when my strength is failing."* (Psalm 71:9 NLT)

"I don't like old people," the young minister said to me as though he expected me to agree. My response was, "Do you realize that in this church, the old people keep the doors open? They are the ones who will pay your salary. Besides, I'm old, so I know where I stand." My comments didn't seem to faze him. I moved on, thinking that all he needed to do was keep on living. My prayer was that God and time would bring a change to his heart. Sadly, he isn't the only under-shepherd who doesn't like old people.

"For the black elderly, there have been few, if any, social, fraternal, or other organizational sources or structures of support. Thus, the roles and potential role of the American church with respect to black seniors is not only pivotal but urgent. Not until the church becomes the astute responder to the needs of those with callused hands, receding hairlines, graying sideburns, fallen arches, stooped backs, and dimming eyesight will the future offer sustained hope for our older members. It behooves the church to remember that, as those who have been willing to 'fight the good fight and finish the race' (see 2 Timothy 4:7), our senior brothers and sisters deserve all of the creativity, compassion, and support we can muster on their behalf."

There are seniors in congregations who suffer at the hands of those too who they have paved paths for and devoted their lives to. Many adult children ignore the parents who sacrificed and struggled to provide for them, raised them as best they could, and did without much of what they needed in order to send them to college. As time passes, sadly, too many elderly parents and grandparents are treated as though they are not affluent enough to warrant the attention of their children and grandchildren. I know seniors who, month after month, do without food and medicine in order to help their adult children and grandchildren. They often sacrifice necessities for cell phones and hairstyles for grandchildren who selfishly show concern for only what they can get. Many seniors pay a high price, hoping for love and attention from those they love unconditionally. They take too long to be loved and given the consideration that apparently heartless family members don't have to give. Dr. Billy Graham said, "All my life, I've been taught how to die, but no one ever taught me how to grow old."

The doors to many black churches would no longer swing open if it were not for the commitment of older members who loved their churches, took pride in them, and believed in giving to sustain the church, even with limited and meager incomes. I still know seniors who give tithes and offerings from the top of all the money they receive, and they feel honored to do so. Few, if any, of them have provisions in wills or endowments for the church. They have done all they could, while they could. What is the responsibility of the church to the seniors who have supported it?

I've spoken with seniors in the church who feel that they are being ignored, mistreated, and forgotten. One member of the same church for nearly 60 years told me, "I love my pastor, but I think he thinks I am stupid. He ignores me, is disrespectful and talks down to me. The only reason I don't say anything is that I have been taught to always respect the pastor. I want him to say something good about me when I die." *Good luck,* I thought. *Sadly, you won't even know.*

A friend of mine cared for her aging mother. Mom's home church was about thirty-five miles from where they lived. She said, "Whenever I would take my mom to her church, and the pastor would look her way and smile to recognize her presence, it would mean the world to her." Another senior said to me, "No one even missed me during my illness. Now that I'm back, they still haven't noticed. I never thought I would be invisible in my own church." All many seniors want is recognition and to be thought about.

There are seniors who have been a part of the same congregation for as long as they can remember. They brought their children up in the church and remained after the children moved on or joined other congregations. I often heard a church member proudly say that she was born into the church she has worshiped in for more than 75 years. "My mother carried me in her belly right here in this church." The church is a familiar place to many seniors, and as friends and relatives die, the church members are the closest many have to family. One Pastor shared with me why he places great importance on the seniors in the congregation he serves. He said that the church needs money to continue serving its members and to finance quality outreach programs. He went on to share what I had never given much thought to at that time, which is that teens and children do not have any money. He said young adults have great responsibilities for children and homes and do not have money. Their responsibilities and priorities are placed elsewhere. In addition, church attendance continues to significantly decline. Many young people who grow up in church leave the church for many years before returning. In my words, I say that seniors in the church can be described as *those who stick and stay.*

"I once was young, but now…" In our youth, we visually see older people, but in our minds, most of us can't imagine ourselves one day wearing and walking in those shoes. According to the U.S. census, about 7,100 people turn 65 years old each day. Many of them grew up in homes where attending church was one of the most important activities of their family. Let us also consider the millions of people over the age of 65 who grew up in the church and continue to hold fast to the institution that has been there for them in one way or another for a lifetime.

Many seniors in the church, facing the issues of aging, find themselves relying on the institution that they know best to assist them in need. They were unable to prepare for retirement due to the challenge of sustaining themselves in the present. With limited means, many of us have had to concentrate on living the best we could in the moments we were in. That means no cushion beyond social security benefits and no comfortable assisted living facilities. Some seniors own homes that are in need of repairs that they cannot afford to make. Affordable housing is minimal and comes with leaving familiar surroundings and neighborhoods. Many seniors could have a better quality of life if there was someone, they could trust to help guide them through the process of change. Without family and or close friends, assistance, and guidance from programs for the elderly, many seniors merely exist. The church can play a role in referring senior members to available services to assist them during this critical season. Churches blessed with financial resources can do more.

Facing reality and obstacles to change can often be an overwhelming challenge. Seniors may no longer be able to drive, prepare meals and keep their houses as they once did. Feelings of inadequacy, loneliness, uselessness, and abandonment often combine to make senior living more difficult. Most of us agree that, in hindsight, we would have done many things differently. With support, many seniors can look forward, celebrating their lives rather than dreading their remaining days. Living with dignity is significant. Respect is imperative. If in no other place, our seniors should be esteemed in the church.

*"Respect the old when you are young. Help the weak when you are strong. Confess your faults when you are wrong. Because one day you will be old, weak and wrong."* (Inspire Quotes)

CHAPTER VI

# Heaven Help Us

*"I was glad when they said unto me, Let us go into the house of the Lord. (Psalm122: I KJV)*

The year was 1980. I was living at Fort Knox, Kentucky, with my husband, a non-commissioned officer stationed at a military army base. I attended the services entitled Fort Knox Gospel Hour. The church was simply called The Chapel. The greatest memory that I have is that everyone came together to worship, and denominations were not an issue. Looking back, it was the Gospel Hour that held my best and most memorable worship experiences. We all just seemed happy to find a place to freely worship, sing, and joyfully praise the Lord. Wednesday evening Bible Study at The Chapel was the highlight of mid-week. I needed words of inspiration and "some church," as we say colloquially, to give me that needed boost to make it to the next service on Sunday.

That Wednesday, I made certain that the house sparkled and that a great dinner was prepared and served. There was no reason for me to stay home. It was time to go to Bible Study. Everything was good until my little girl, and I started to leave. As I picked up my Bible and my purse, my husband grabbed my arm and quietly but threateningly said, "If you go to that church, I am going to come there, drag you out, and stomp a mud hole in your a__." What would it be like to have such a hole stomped in any part of me, I thought? This was not the first time he had made this threat. Though I was afraid, I tried hard not to show it. I responded softly, "Okay, I will see you when you get there." I knew that it really angered him when I did not show fear, cry, or curl up in a corner. One Sunday morning, I even crawled into a closet, where I stayed for more than an hour because he threatened to do me harm if I went to church. This time I continued to move toward the door. It was not my intention to further upset him, but I could not continue to coward down and live with daily fright, especially when I so firmly believed that going to church on Sunday and one hour on Wednesday evening was doing nothing wrong. I had to do something for esteem in my moments of self-disappointment. I was in an abusive marriage for the second time.

As I drove off, I trembled so hard that it seemed that the steering wheel would come unhinged. In spite of my brave face, I was scared, really scared. My greatest fear was that someday my husband would carry out his threats, attack and beat me unmercifully, or kill me and the children as he threatened.

I safely arrived at Bible Study and sat on the front row of the church. I found it hard to concentrate on the lesson. Blinded by the quiet tears that streamed down my face, I was unable to read. I saw the Pastor as he moved and stood in the hallway that faced where my daughter and I were sitting. He gestured for me to come into the hallway. He asked, "Why are you crying, Sister Allen? It can't be because of Bible Study," he said with humor in his voice. I told him about the threat that my husband made to come to the church and stomp me. He responded with, "Get your purse and your Bible. You and your daughter go home. Have you seen the size of his feet?" the Pastor said with humor in his voice. My husband wore size 14 EEE shoes.

I got my things and held the hand of my five-year-old. The Pastor walked us through the back door of the church and assisted us in getting into the car. When I arrived home, my husband seemed genuinely glad to see us. He acted as though nothing had ever happened. One of us had won another round.

Instead of helping me to work through the threats and take a stand against the violence of my husband, my very own Pastor enabled the abuse, pressing me to go home, leave the assumed safety of the church, and go back to the suffering that caused me so much pain. I was so confused. Just maybe that was the best course of action at the time.

For years, I smiled when I thought about how the Pastor handled this situation, only to one day realize that it was not funny. At the time, the Pastor was a young Captain/Chaplain, a recent seminary graduate, and this was his first congregation. Obviously, the seminary had not taught him how to handle domestic violence among the congregants he served. It comes as no surprise that the male dominance that appears in the Bible prevents many men and women in ministry from understanding and accepting the severity and reality of domestic violence in the church. Many years later, I spent four and a half years in seminary, and the topic of domestic violence against women within faith communities and how ministers and Pastors should handle these situations was never taught to me either. In fact, domestic violence was never even a topic of class discussion.

One Sunday, while at Fort Knox, I stood with the choir singing the solo I had practiced for weeks. I looked toward the church's open door, and there my husband stood in the foyer with folded arms staring at me. He was a big guy, about six-foot-three and close to 300 pounds. It seemed that an instant lump the size of a lemon swelled in my throat. The words of the song became frozen in my fears. As the tears rolled down my face, I softly said, "Jesus, Jesus," as I remembered that a counselor had assured me that the men in the church would not let my husband's threat of dragging me out become a reality. I continued singing with my eyes closed, and when I opened them, my husband was gone. I tried consoling myself with the thought that maybe I was just imagining it all. My heart pounded rapidly as I drove home that afternoon. I didn't know what to expect. When I walked in the door, my husband unpredictably said, "Yeah, you sounded pretty good up there singing this morning." I just smiled and quietly said, "Thank you." Inside, I wanted to shout. This time I won, if there was such a thing as winning. There was one fear that I didn't have, and that was that my husband would come into the church and shoot me and others as was happening in the news. He actually hated guns even after spending nearly eighteen years in the military, but then, of course, we can never be sure. I came to understand that the psychological fear he implanted was just as menacing as any other form of violence.

Fortunately, the Pastor whose presence in my life became so valuable, swiftly became a wiser man. I believe he began to interact with his more experienced colleagues and developed a greater awareness of domestic violence. Through counseling, he provided immeasurable support. He later rendered resources that helped me to safely leave my abusive marriage. Though I sat in "Pew Pain" every Wednesday and Sunday in that church for more than a year, it was where I felt safest. Since that time, I have sat in many pews in many churches. I have hurt through my anxieties and fears, through illness, disappointment, unemployment, pending evictions, and contemplating homelessness. However, through my pain, I learned to be more appreciative of my plight. Never since have I suffered or feared an abusive relationship, nor threatened harm because I wanted to go to church.

The acts of domestic violence that occur inside the walls of faith communities are represented by staggering, terrifying statistics. The legendary Christian leader Chuck Colson (1931-2012) once said, "Tragically, studies reveal that spousal abuse is just as common within the evangelical churches as anywhere else. This means that about 25 percent of Christian homes witness abuse of some kind."

True congregational care demands an awareness of violence against women within and outside of our churches. Those in ministry should be taught and prepared to act to prevent this violence, rather than reacting after it occurs. Worse yet, it is too often shamefully ignored. I've heard stories from women in the ministry of all kinds of abuse and assaults that in comparison, make the things that happened to me seem almost like child's play. I was told by two women in ministry who reported physical abuse by their husbands to their male superiors, "Go home and forget about it." The greatest similarity of abused women is survival.

Though they may not call it hate, the misogynous mindsets of men have long existed. In the church, women are socially discriminated against and too often oppressed. Even in this day and age, it is exceptional when women have major organizational and spiritual roles, in some denominations. The Bible records stories from which many men take their Q's and continue to develop flawed mindsets and behaviors that are inflected upon the women who line the pews, support the programs, and pay the salaries of the men in leadership. The respect that women have earned should be given to them in the church. Realistically, the same people on the outside of the church are the ones on the inside who bring with them the abusive use of a kind of power that would be accepted in no other place. In the Old Testament, women were considered property. Even if such behaviors were a way of life at another time in Biblical history, that time has passed. We must fast forward. There must be changes in accepted behaviors, attitudes and actions as they relate to the treatment of women.

Read the story of Tamar found in II Samuel 13:1-22; the story of the incestuous rape of a young woman by her brother. It is not recorded that King David, the father did anything in response to such a painful and demoralizing assault upon his daughter. The Bible tells us that David was "very wroth", meaning having extreme anger but tells us nothing more. Absalom, the brother of Tamar and another son of the king demonstrated uncontrollable rage and sought revenge upon the rapist of his sister. This is a story of crime, power, control, victimization, and the emotions of all involved. It is the story of a father who aided and abetted in the crime by doing nothing. Though disturbed, the advice that the brother Absalom gave his sister was to hold her peace [because] it is your brother. (II Samuel 13:30) I've read five translations that say nearly the same, that Tamar was to take lightly the matter given her relationship with her abuser. Little consolation was given to a woman who suffered and was shamed. Absalom had his bother killed sometime later. Suffering in silence seems to have been the cavalier attitude in the day of Tamar. That same attitude too often exists today.

We can only speculate as to why David the King, the father of Tamar, did nothing about the rape of his daughter by his son. Did he accept the wrong? Was he ashamed of his indiscretions and, therefore, chose silence?

Was he living with what he may have believed to be generational father-to-son behavior where a man can take what he wants from a woman at any cost? Was keeping shame from his son more important than the pain and shame his daughter suffered? Was Tamar and the pain she suffered of great embarrassment to her father? Avoiding the matters of rape and incest in the church will not make them vanish! The silence only worsens, wrongfully continues, and exacerbates these painful situations.

Wearing a clergy collar has not stopped men from being abusers. Domestic violence lurks in the church too often, starting from the pulpit. Physical, mental, and verbal abuse greatly exist in the lives of too many men of God, the people they live with, and those who believe in them. Abusive male pastors have difficulty speaking up on behalf of women who listen to their sermons and pay their salaries because of the shoes they walk in. They refuse to address the mistreatment of women in their congregations because the behaviors of abusive men too often mirror their own. Then there are the women who choose not to hold these men responsible. This is a true story of the preacher who beat his wife and was incarcerated for the crime. Upon release, he went to the church leaders and demanded his salary for the time he was in jail. I am not aware of what his contract stated, but the male leaders refused to pay him. He threatened to sue the church. The church members, mostly women, took a vote. It was decided that he should be paid and reinstated as pastor. "He's a good man, and we all make mistakes," they said. The definition of a good man and good leader is flawed, in my opinion. So much for the women who think that the Pastor is all but walks on water.

Numerous articles have been written about preying pastors, and we're not talking about praying on their knees. Too many pastors have been known to have affairs with female members who seek them for counseling and help during the times when they, as members, are in crisis and most vulnerable. There are people who require help but do not come forth because they are embarrassed and have not been given the respect of privacy. The appalling and sinful behaviors of religious leaders must not be overlooked or accepted with the excuse that *we all make* mistakes, giving them permission to repeat the behavior. There must be ways to hold ministers to higher moral standards rather than the defense *he's just a man*. As for women everywhere, when you know in your very being that God has truly given you value, you will give respect and demand respect.

No price tag is too large for some women to pay for the privilege of being the wife of the Pastor. Being the first lady comes with prestige, presents, and the extra paycheck their husbands get for playing the caring pastor role. They get to be seen in public and go home in a fine car with the man that other women admire and swoon to be with. "The time he spends at church, he could be somewhere with me," one Pastor's wife said to me. She went on to say that all the gifts the people give her are well deserved for having to put up with them. The material girls and those filled with greed are not about to give that up. Being treated like trash is the accepted tradeoff for what some call benefits. There are Pastors who stand in pulpits and preach to their wives and mistresses, both with their children sitting beside them, in the same church during the same service. Talk about a tangled web!

There are exceptional and positive first ladies who do not need the hovering of church members to validate them. They have their own careers as well as work in the church. They dress appropriately, speak wisely, demonstrate good character, and refuse to take part in church drama. Most of all, they make their pastor/husbands and the church proud. Being the wife of a pastor and leading in the church beside him is a calling. A good Pastor and wife team is a blessing to a congregation and the people of God.

This is the story of my maternal grandmother's best friend. For more than fifty years, they were inseparable. They attended church, raised their children together, and shared life's situations. Ms. Ann, as we will call her, was a very petite and pretty lady. In her day, she could have been described as a trophy. She was a good woman, well-liked, and highly respected.

A recently widowed pastor pursued her and convinced her they could enjoy a very good life and live out their senior years comfortably. He planned that they could reside in the church parsonage, have someone to come in to do the housework, travel, and enjoy their golden years. They both were close to seventy years old. The marriage was short-lived. They were only weeks into the marriage when he became physically abusive. She made it clear that a man had never hit her and wasn't about to accept it at this stage of her life. She let him know that he didn't have enough to offer her in exchange for abuse and that the fact that he was a well-respected minister did not matter. She wasted no time leaving him and moved back into the home she owned, which her daughter and grandchildren were occupying. She immediately got legal advice, and the marriage was resolved quickly.

I admired her fortitude. Still, at her age, she had her pride and principles. She refused to accept abuse or to keep the behavior of the elderly preacher a secret. Her well-being mattered most. We don't want to imagine domestic violence among the elderly, but it is a harsh reality that we must face. How long had this pastor fooled his members into believing that he was just a nice little old man of God? I find it hard to believe that his abusive behavior began at such a late stage in life. We will never know for sure. He likely abused his first wife. Who knows what mask they both wore?

Age is not a precursor to abuse in the church. There are senior women in the pews who, despite appearance, continue to be in horrible marriages. Some of them live with men who would still sleep with every woman who would have them, except that father time prevents. Many women have spent sleepless nights waiting for husbands to come home tired, drunk, penniless, and sometimes bringing with them children from their affairs that their wives then have to take care of. There are older men in the church who control every penny, often subjecting the woman who has lived a lifetime with them and their foolishness to suffer quietly in lack. It is said, "Ain't no fool like an old fool.' So, she sits Sunday after Sunday with the belief that one of them will die first, and that will make the difference.

How does the church respond to violence against women? No response is a response. "As long as the church is quiet in a world that resonated with the cries of abused women, it is failing in its ministry of reconciliation. It is simply functioning as a sounding brass and a clanging cymbal… The church is called to bind up the bruises of women who have suffered not only from the violence of their spouses but all of the passive violence of a church which has failed to recognize their situation and intervene on their behalf."

Men in ministry, male leaders, and men in general in the church would benefit from sensitivity training. I have spoken with men in the church about rape, incest, domestic violence and abuse. The responses have ranged from nothingness to one man saying, "Women just ought to just get over it." One pastor and I had conflicting views about a wife who called 911 when her husband became verbally abusive and physically threatening. The pastor said her calls were premature. We disagreed on the timing as she had previously been a victim of domestic violence at the hands of her husband and feared it happening again. We served the same congregation and preached from the same pulpit but saw so many things differently. "In matters of principle stand like a rock; in matters of taste, swim with the current." (Thomas Jefferson) It is great when ministers and assistants are on the same page regarding issues that they both hold strong beliefs about. I find myself both standing and swimming.

> *"You may encounter many defeats, but you may not be defeated. In fact, it may be necessary to encounter the defeats, so you can know who you are, what you can rise from, how you can still come out of it"*
> – Maya Angelou

## CHAPTER VII

# Bullies Everywhere

*"…You shall love your neighbor as yourself"*
*(Matthew 22:39)*

There are bullies in the church. They are the women who take advantage of every opportunity to mistreat other women in the church. Though we say we want others to join us, there are women who seemingly can't wait to demonstrate their territorial stance rather than being welcoming. They take advantage of every opportunity to oppress and intimidate other women, giving little or no thought to where they have come from and how God has so accepted them.

Church is probably one of the few places many women can get away with atrocious actions: throw stones and hide their hands. Some women must mark their territories with abrasive behaviors, especially in the church kitchen. Bad actions are often tolerated because the church is supposed to be a forgiving place. Bad behavior is just wrong, and when it happens in the church, it negatively reflects our understanding of Biblical teaching. We say we want the body of Christ to grow, and too often, when new people come, they are ignored or mistreated. Given the gender gap, new church participants are most often women. We should want more than empty seats filled and offerings. The welcoming committee should be sincere in welcoming and including everyone.

Perhaps too many women have not been taught or learned to love themselves and may find it even harder to love their neighbor. In our lack of self-love, we too often accept being put down and not taking a stand when mistreated. Many leaders teach submissiveness, from which we form excuses to accept being mistreated. Women who stand for what is right in the church are often, unfortunately, negatively considered and branded as troublemakers. So, accepting being the victim is a weak excuse to do little other than quietly suffer. Is it that we believe that there is redemption in our suffering?

Once, as a new member, one of the associate ministers and a student in the seminary, the Pastor asked me to help him organize the agenda for a church meeting. We discussed the items as well as anticipated responses. Days later, during that meeting, I commented on one of the topics. One of the members responded with hateful disrespect. I was quickly ignored as others spoke up and were treated differently. Following the meeting, as I walked to my car, that church member walked up to me and, with an undefinable attitude, said, "What you had to say was good, and it made sense. Maybe someone will listen to you if you stay here long enough." She immediately turned and walked away. I later learned that she was a front-runner of the small group that ran everything at that church. The pastor went along for the ride. More importantly, I learned this was not an exceptional situation, as many leaders could care less about who runs things as long as they pick up their paycheck. "If you manage to stay here long enough, maybe someone will listen to you" is the line that spoke volumes. The church, too often, is run like a secret society with rituals for acceptance requiring initiation.

A few years later, as an ordained Associate Minister at another church, one of the members, in what I thought was a friendly conversation, asked, "What are the things you would like to do as a minister in this church?" Thinking she cared, I happily started talking about outreach programs and organizing groups for seniors and women. These were things the Pastor and I had previously discussed. The long-time member said, "Well, why don't you find another church where you can do all that!" This was the person who threw the rocks at others in the church and hid her hand behind her back. As a retired social worker, she was highly critical of what everyone else did in the church and only participated in or supported if it was her idea or her family and friends were involved. Her conduct was not exceptional. Sadly, there are women everywhere in churches with the same kinds of behavior. Rather than sharing the gifts God has blessed them with to be a blessing to the Body of Christ, they are selfishly critical. Even though I served at the pleasure of the Pastor, I was still an outsider.

"When the power of love overcomes the love of power the world will know peace," said Jimi Hendrix. The presence of each new person initiates changes. Our prayer should be for good change as we grow and become the people who make God proud. Many of us find comfort zones in church, good or not-so-good, and we don't want to change or lose a false sense of power.

I have yet to understand the viciousness and lack of unity and feelings of some women toward one another in the church. I've watched as sisters with the same parents come to the same church year after year and refuse to acknowledge the presence of one another or even speak. I have watched as sisters who grew up in the same household and same church clawed at each other like savage beasts following morning service as they stood in the church. There are cliques and sororities in the church. If a woman is a part of one of them, she can be accepted and included. Now, if a woman is her own person without group dependency, she may never be called off the bench, included, recognized, or even given the respect she deserves.

Beginning in the book of Genesis, there are stories of oppression and mistreatment of women. Females were considered to be property, tools for bartering, and insignificant human beings except for male pleasures. While sadly, this is Biblical history, the horror stories of domination and deceit should have no place in the thinking as examples of how women should be thought of and treated today.

October is Domestic Violence Awareness Month. The speaker for that Sunday morning was a church member who had recently earned her Ph.D. in an area of study far from religion. Her accomplishment was major for anyone and even more so for someone who grew up in a small, often challenged community. The speaker was quite aware of the issues facing the group to which she spoke, many of whom were family members. Some of us seem to forget where we come from and forget to praise God for our promotions.

Most of us have read or heard at least part of the story in the 29th Chapter of Genesis. It sounds like one of the greatest love stories of the ages from across the pulpit. However, there is more to the story. What is shared and remembered most is that Jacob worked seven years to marry the woman of his dreams, Rachel. It is a Bible family narrative about two sisters, their father, and Jacob, the man who married both.

The speaker verbally painted pictures of both sisters. The negative picture was painted of the sister Rachel, who was unhappy because her father gave her sister to the man she expected to marry. The older sister, Leah, was in trickery, given that the bride was to be commended according to the speaker. Though she was not the pretty of the two sisters, she had the best attitude; according to the speaker, "Your attitude determines your altitude" was the widely used quote. According to the speaker, Rachel had a bad attitude and should have kept quiet. In other words, speaking up about the abusive behavior of her father was wrong.

This thought projection was alarming, especially from a woman across the pulpit on a Sunday morning. Remaining quiet about abuse is another means of control. We've heard the statement: "What goes on in this house stays in this house" or "This is between us." The women who are threatened and subjected to silence continue to suffer without support, often sadly believing that they are responsible. Accepting abuse does not come with a badge of honor. While the actions in these stories were culturally accepted in their time, we must be careful not to suggest, subject, or accept the negative behaviors of another era in society today. What happened in these Old Testament chapters should guide us through the *thou shall nots* for this time we live.

The stories in Chapters 29-31 of Genesis are those of love, pain, incest, greed, and deceit. How these stories esteem women is a matter of interpretation. To briefly summarize, Jacob sees a woman at the well with flocks of sheep. He falls in love with her and seeks her hand from her father, his uncle, making the woman he loves his first cousin. The mother of Jacob and Laban and the father of the daughters are sister and brother. In response to the request, Laban says, "I'd rather give her to you than someone outside the family" (Genesis 29:19 Living Bible). Jacob agrees to seven years of labor to have the woman he loves. Upon the completed agreement, the father, Laban, tricks Jacob into marrying Leah, the older sister. When Jacob discovers the deception, the father tells him that he will have to work another seven years but gives him Rachel, the younger daughter of his choice, after the week of the marriage celebration. Jacob now has two wives, his first cousins and their handmaidens Bilhah and Zilpah, who also became Jacob's wives. In just a short time, Jacob now has four wives. Jacob fathered a total of twelve children with these four women. Leah always hoped for love and bore the babies of the man who loved her sister, Rachel. Rachel, the wife Jacob labored for, desperately wanted to be the bearer of the bloodline of Jacob. She had difficulties conceiving.

The children of Leah, Rachel, and Jacob are siblings and cousins. Their aunts are married to their father, and their father is also their second cousin. The children's grandfather is also their great-uncle. Imagine the family reunion. The Bible mentions one girl child born to Leah named Dinah. She is the first daughter in the Bible whose name is mentioned at birth.

Leah, the older sister and first wife, is said to be the less attractive of the two. Some writers say that her appearance kept her humble and meek. However, her marriage was part of a scheme and web of dishonesty for all involved. Was she willing to go to any lengths for a husband? Was she forcefully made to be with the man who wanted her sister? Did she have a choice in the matter? She, however, loved her husband and had a rival relationship with her sister, whom her husband favored.

Here were two sisters in competition for the love of the same man. We can only imagine the problems in this polygamous household. Leah has children who believe that Jacob would love her more. Eventually, Rachel had a son and died in childbirth with a second child. Undoubtedly, both women suffered immense emotional pain due to the abusive behaviors of their father and their husband. However, prior to leaving the land of their father, the sisters united in their belief that their father sold them and cheated them and his grandchildren of their parts of the inheritance.

The speaker stressed that, in her opinion, Rachel was punished by God with barrenness and death in childbirth because of her negative attitude. She said that Leah ultimately won, outliving Rachel, and therefore had the honor of being buried next to her husband, Jacob. While the burial place may have been significant, I question the winning.

On this Sunday in 2013, Domestic Violence Month, women were being told to be quiet and accept the pains of injustices and humiliation and that to do so demonstrates boldness, strength, and character. One officer of the church said to me regarding the incestuous rape of a stepdaughter and impregnation of a minor by a minister in the church, "I don't know why women want to make an issue of this stuff. Just forget it and move on." Following brief incarceration, all was forgiven, and the minister was allowed to continue in his position in the church.

Abuse is taken lightly by too many men and accepted by too many women in the church, the place where we are supposed to work diligently at getting it as close to right as possible. Any responsibility for wrongdoing by the men in this Biblical story was ignored by the woman bringing the message that Sunday, who obviously thinks abusing women as well as women accepting abuse is alright. This story was an extremely bad frame of reference from the pulpit or any place to suggest how women of today should see themselves. Accepting abuse is never honorable.

In my fury, I went to the Pastor of the church. I first asked his opinion of the message. He told me he thought it was good except for being too long. I asked if he thought it was negative, and he said, "No." Had we heard the same sermon? I proceeded to tell him exactly what I thought. His response was, "Well, the speaker does have a Ph.D." I said, "That doesn't make her a theologian. A geologist with a Ph.D. cannot perform brain surgery simply because he or she is a doctor." How was Rachel supposed to feel knowing that her husband was having baby after baby with her sister? I asked anxiously, seeking his response. In defense of it all, the Pastor reminded me that writing a sermon can be difficult for anyone, even those trained in ministry. My conversation with the pastor gave me increased insight into what he thought about women. And so, the suffering too often continues as too many women are devalued.

That Sunday, I sat in Pew Pain, hurting all of the women who listened with the belief that they needed to suffer in silence. I wanted to walk out of the church and wished that, in solidarity, other women would get up and walk out, too, refusing to listen to another word of insane advice. However, I knew that staying would help me gain greater insight into the speaker's mind. The more I heard, the more alarmed I became with the opportunity the speaker took to be oppressive. I prayed that the women who listened would think for themselves and find value in their greatness.

I believe that church leaders have a responsibility to ensure sound teaching and that they are responsible for what comes across the pulpits. Corrections should be made when unjust words and harm are done to the people. Many people are bruised, believing they must accept whatever is said through a preached word. No one should be mistreated in or out of the church. Degrees, occupations, or financial contributions to the church should give the pastor or anyone designated such rights.

Bullying in the church, just as in any other place, should be called out for how wrong it is. The perception of social power, superiority, and intimidation should not exist in the church. Let us not be like bull sharks that latch on with sharp, deadly teeth of mean spirit-ness. Let us be mindful that church should be the place where we demonstrate the love of God. It should be where we help strengthen and nourish one another.

> Kindness *"People who treat other people as less than human must not be surprised when the bread they cast on the waters comes floating back to them poisoned"* (James A. Baldwin)

## CHAPTER VIII

# From the Pew To the Pulpit

*"And it shall come to pass in the last days, saith God, I will pour out of my Spirit upon all flesh: and your sons and your daughters shall prophesy..."* (Acts 2:17 KJV)

I always thought I would be the preacher's wife, never the preacher. Being a minister of the Gospel from the pulpit in front of a church was not my plan. It takes some of us a while to accept that God's plans will always supersede our plans. God spoke to me, called my name, and gave me directions. I knew it was God but doubted my abilities and obviously lacked the faith I needed.

Without any doubt, I heard the voice of God say, "Preach My Word." When I attempted to dismiss what I heard God say, He called my name, "Alexis, Preach My Word." For more than thirty years, I refused to do what God directed. I had unimaginable excuses, and life didn't go as I thought it should. My sister is a minister, my daughter is a minister, and my niece is a minister. "Come on, God," I said. "That's enough women in one family." Besides, in my narrow-minded thinking, I wondered *who would listen to me*. Finally, I could no longer run. I graduated from Hood Theological Seminary, Salisbury, NC, in 2009. I was honored to receive

The George Clayton Tharrington Memorial Award, presented to "the senior student who best exemplifies the outstanding preaching qualities of Reverend Tharrington. These qualities include Biblical preaching with evangelistic emphasis, keen imagination, creative homiletics, and extemporaneous style." God had listeners. I told God, but it was God who told me!

The Bible tells us that God created man and woman in His image. (Gen 1:27) While this is a biblical truth, in the hearts and minds of so many men and women, equality and opportunity for women should not and does not exist in ministry. Ministry is a male-dominated profession, often precluding many opportunities for women to serve the people of God. Increasingly, more women are earning Master's and Doctoral degrees in ministry that qualify them for leadership in Christian Ministry. Many women have fought for the right to do what God called them despite the challenges and lack of acceptance. Numerous denominations refused to license women to preach the Gospel, leading to many non-affiliated Pentecostal and Holiness female preachers. At my age, professional ministry was relatively new to me. I was discouraged by the many injustices I observed and read about.

In the winter of 2018, I was blessed to be a part of a group of Hood Theological Seminary students and alumni who went to Kingston, Jamaica, to study the History of Religion In the Caribbean. We resided and studied at the United Theological College of the West Indies (UTCWI). The experience was planned and arranged by Dr. Sharon Grant, a professor of the history of Christianity at Hood Theological Seminary. During one of our discussion lunches, I had the pleasure of being seated next to one of our tour guides, a young minister who graduated from the seminary where we studied. As a very dedicated young man to his calling, he served four churches and traveled four days each week to give each church and the people the best care possible. We explored a number of topics, including women in ministry. He said that the biggest problem is that women ministers are too often rejected and disrespected by the women of the church for no reason other than they are used to having men to minister them. This is a universal issue. With little regard for the fact that there are women who are well trained, have great skills, and care about them, there are women who refuse to hear the Word of God from a woman. Once, a woman in the church said to me, "I really don't have anything personal against women preaching, but Paul said women should be quiet in the church." What Paul said is often and purposefully taken out of context and misunderstood to suggest that women should not be in public ministry.

The reference of the Apostle Paul telling the women in the Corinthian church to be quiet (1 Corinthian 14:34-35) should be placed in context. The church of Corinth was one noted for confusion and disorder. During one such time, the women were told to be quiet and to speak with their husbands about matters outside the church. The women sat separately from the men and were given a patriarchal order. Surely, there should always be respect for the House of God, and leadership is responsible for setting expectations. Further, it should be noted that the Apostle Paul is credited for 13 books of the New Testament, referred to as the Pauline Epistles. Each was written to address a specific church and the concerns of that congregation.

"My God, that woman can preach! She preaches just like a man." One of the male preachers made this comment about a female preacher. She was very pleased as she accepted his enthusiasm and remarks as outstanding accolades. She was loud, whooped, and sometimes sounded as though she was having an asthma attack. Many women preach messages from the pulpit that are neither masculine nor feminine in delivery. They preach the word of God without theatrical tactics that are sometimes considered a part of male preaching. I don't preach like a man. I preach like me, giving the word of God to the people of God as God directs. I used to jokingly say to the guys in seminary, "I don't have a whoop, I'm not loud, and I don't spin around, wave, or throw my handkerchief."

I served at First Calvary Baptist Church in Winston Salem, North Carolina, for more than six years. It was a predominantly geriatric congregation. The men were real gentlemen, and the women dressed tastefully and wore beautiful hats. They were ladies. I thought little of it when one of the deacons was waiting as I left the pulpit one Sunday following service. One of the men would often wait to take my Bible or belongings as I came down the five steps. I appreciated this kindness. However, this time it was different. The deacon, a tall man heavy in stature, said in his thunderous voice, "Rev Allen, if Rev. Wilson was here, you wouldn't be preaching from his pulpit!" Though I was unexpectedly surprised, I softly replied, "All due respect, Deacon, I didn't know Rev. Wilson. However, I was told that he was the Pastor here for many years and died more than fifteen years ago. I'd like us to think of this pulpit as the platform of God." Rev. Wilson had been the church's beloved pastor for a long time. His memory was very much present, especially for many members who grew up under his ministry.

There are men in ministry who very much respect and support the contributions of women in ministry. Rev. Calvin Runnels was one of them. I was ordained with full rights in ministry by the High Point Educational and Missionary Baptist Association on July 24th, 2008. My pastor, Rev. Calvin Runnels, was scheduled to leave with many of our church members for a trip to his home church in Chicago where his father was the pastor. Rev. Runnels changed his plans, saw his family and members off, and stayed to support me. After congratulating me and giving me his fresh white handkerchief, we shared tears of joy at the accomplishment. He said, "You've done it, and I'm proud of you. I'm leaving for Chicago in the morning." I responded, "Who will be in charge of the church and the service on Sunday with you, your assistant, and most of the church officers out of town?" "You will," he replied with a broad smile. "You've just been ordained." He walked off with his quick and deliberate steps. He turned and, as he walked away, said, "I'll see you next week."

My heart pounded with anxiety, honor, and joy. My Pastor was entrusting to me the church and the congregation he so proudly and assiduously served. At that moment, I realized the importance he'd placed on study, discipline, order, presentation, commitment, and hard work during the past year of Supervised Ministry. He was preparing me for a woman in ministry he could be proud of. He trusted me, and this opportunity was given to me to display my gifts. My struggling sense of inner confidence began to struggle a little less. Years have passed, and I have never had another Pastor who has given me such guidance, respect, or opportunity.

Rev. Runnels has gone to be with the Lord. I so appreciate God placing him in my life. He has been the most encouraging person in my ministry. He demonstrated belief in me when I found it hard to believe in myself.

God truly blessed that Sunday. Many gathered from several states for a family reunion. However, countless members were out of town, and all the visitors made up for them. Most importantly, the sermon spoke to the heart of the people. A circle of people gathered around to talk to me following the service and to thank me for the message and warm reception they received as visitors. They didn't seem to mind that the message came from a woman. Mostly, I was blessed because of the Word God had given me to give His people. One of my female colleagues and Sister in Ministry often reminds me, "It was a woman who first carried the Gospel as she carried Jesus in her womb."

Some denominations widely limit or omit the positions of women. The fact that they have studied and earned theological degrees is seemingly irrelevant. For three of my years in seminary, I was blessed by the presence of a young colleague who came directly from college. She was bright, energetic and bubbly. It was a real joy to be in her presence. She often helped me to forget the gravity of the task that often seemed so difficult. Most of all, she loved God and His people. Though her workload was nonetheless of anyone else's, she somehow found the time to do whatever she could for others. A few days before graduation, she came to me with seriousness and an expression of hopelessness. She said that she had to accept that it didn't matter what she achieved, she could never be anything more in her denomination than a missionary. She was torn, knowing that to stay at the church and in the denomination she loved, she would not be able to use the theological degree she had worked so hard for. Some ten years later, I spoke with her. Though she has moments of nostalgia, she has moved on and is serving in another denomination.

Fortunately, some men believe that the needs of the people are great, that there is so much work to be done, and that God chooses whoever God wants to do that work. I have been privileged to meet several men in ministry with whom I share philosophies. Recently, I spoke with a male colleague, an ordained minister in the Lutheran church, who shared that he fought very hard for more than twenty-five years to have a female minister on staff. He had been a member of the church for more than forty years. He was vigorously opposed for his beliefs and suggestions. Many years later, and with a female minister on staff, many members repeatedly thank him for his stand. They say, "We just didn't consider how differently women handle issues and their diverse points of view. We've always been so used to male leadership." The support of these male leaders continues to be encouraging. There are still churches where women in ministry are not allowed in the pulpit and must sit on the front row while their husbands are accepted and serve from the platform. While the acceptance of women in ministerial roles is changing, it still has a way to go.

Many secure male leaders in ministry wholly accept women in ministry and appreciate their presence and service. There are places where we can serve God, be of service to the ministry and fellowship, and receive sound teaching and support. We are not condemned to bad situations in the church. It is a choice. One of my sisters in the ministry says this to women in the pulpit and the pew, "Staying in an abusive church is like staying in an abusive relationship, believing that you have no way out or no place to go should you escape." She is a voice of experience.

Integrity is too often traded for a place on the pulpit and an opportunity to preach on occasion. Many women in ministry do not speak up for fear of losing whatever privileges male-dominated ministries allow them. They keep the secrets of pastors' domestic abuse, adultery, stealing, and wrongs in exchange for a place on the pulpit. We don't want to talk about how often women in ministry do the work of their male counterparts and are given little or no credit. It is embarrassing that the religion and the church that we embrace continue to disrespect our God-given gifts, talents, and education. How women are treated in ministry is not a topic to be approached with anger or indignity, but rather factually as we work toward respect, solutions, and equity. Women in ministry must always be mindful of the reason they have been called.

Each of us in ministry must be held to accountability standards. As women, we have a responsibility to present ourselves with the appearance of godliness in the pew and in the pulpit as well as set examples for other women. We all seek attention. When, where, and how we get that attention should be well thought out. The pulpit is not the place for the tightest skirt, five-inch heels, and dresses so tight that every pimple is outlined. Nails should not be too long to turn the pages of the Bible. The pulpit is the place to promote God and God only. Be the woman of God that He and His people can be proud of.

*"Real change, enduring change, happens one step at a time."*
Ruth Bader Ginsburg

*"Passion is the log that keeps the fire of purpose blazing."*
Oprah Winfrey

CHAPTER IX

# Congregational Care

*"And now beware! Be sure that you feed and shepherd God's flock—his church, purchased with his blood—for the Holy Spirit is holding you responsible as overseers.* (Acts20:28 The Living Bible)

The issues of life direct us to pews on Sunday. We come with the hopes of finding spiritual ointments, sometimes for temporary relief and injuries, and sometimes for deep wounds that all but consume us. Life is what happens when the flames of the candles are extinguished, and we are told to "go in peace." Peace may be the least of what we find beyond the temporary sanctuary that may have offered a brief refuge. Caring for the people of God should not begin at the eleven o'clock hour and end following an emotional message, a mighty praise, and a departing benediction.

How do we address the concerns that bring people into the house of God seeking solutions to the challenges of daily life? What are our responsibilities to them beyond the moments when we stand before them and above them, looking down from our pulpit pedestals? It is important that we provide care after the benediction.

"We must care for the soul and the soles." I read this line somewhere and couldn't agree more. We need both physical and spiritual care. While the first obligation of the church is spiritual, when feet are bare, and stomachs gurgle with the sounds and pains of hunger, physical needs must be met. It is hard for most of us to be guided or concentrate on any beliefs when we are severely hurt. The church is bigger than the building and must go far beyond the brick-and-mortar structure to care for the people. Everyone is in need of care. Whatever our levels of independence or resources, we have been created to live in need of the gifts of one another. We are blessed to be a blessing. Some of us have been blessed with strength, some with education, and some with wealth, resources, and possessions. There is the strength of youth and the wisdom of the old among us. When we share our gifts, the benefits increase for all.

The Bible tells us, "But Moses' hands grew weary, so they took a stone and put it under him, and he sat on it, while Aaron and Hur held up his hands, one on one side, and the other on the other side. So his hands were steady until the going down of the sun." (Exodus 17:12) Moses received the help that he needed for the good of the cause. We, too, need help as we face the frailties of life that can consume us. From the cradle to the grave, we live needing care, support, and concern from others.

One of my Pastoral Care and Counseling courses was titled Equipping Persons for Trans-formative Leadership in Christian Ministry. Portions of a submitted paper are included. Required readings and classroom lectures spurred intense thought for the need to better prepare as ministers to effectively care for the people of God. The many obligations of a ministry, combined with bivocations, often cause leaders to lose sight or face difficulties prioritizing congregation ministerial obligations. Pastoral Care is not the calling of every Pastor. The following statement, without question, validates the great and immediate need for Pastoral Care and Counseling.

*"...the only relevance that really matters is the deep needs of persons- relevance to the places in their lives where they hurt and hope, curse and pray, hunger for meaning and thirst for significant relationships."*

This statement followed a parable of the changes, attitudes, and structure of what started out as a lifesaving station on a dangerous seacoast. Enthusiasm for the original objective to rescue shipwrecked people remained for some and undoubtedly, intentions were good. However, as more people came to help, bringing with them individual mindsets and assorted values, change was inevitable. Many of those who had been rescued wanted to become members of the group and help with rescues. Others thought that the facility needed greater aesthetics and increased comfort. Given the conditions of those being rescued, some of the rescuers elected to install outside showers. The rescue station became a clubhouse. Thus, one new clubhouse and then another rose along the seashore.

The parable is an analogy to the present-day saving stations that we call churches. Does the church really welcome the smelly, confused, and often disoriented shipwrecked survivors who come from the stormy seas of life, or would the church rather they shower outside? Does the church continue to build new structures of separatism? Is the church concerned with "the only relevance that matters...?" Cinbelle stated that through Pastoral Care and Counseling, the church stays relevant to human needs. It remains a lifesaving station, a hospital, a garden of spiritual life, and not a museum. (Clinbell p. 14)

The certainty of change as the seconds of our lives evolve into moments in which we breathe speaks volumes. No two moments are ever the same. As harsh of a reality as this may be, it must be grasped. If not, as caregivers, we will expect that we need not change our minds or our methods. Responses to the needs of the people must be relevant. As those of us receiving care (and we all need it), living in our past can prevent us from living with rich and abundant present blessings and celebrating the now gifts of God. We need help to move from past negatives to present positives and future potentials.

Fragmented, broken people often need more help than they know and more help than we are willing and capable as ministers to give. Therefore, the concept of community is paramount in working toward wholeness as we respect individualism, strongly bearing in mind that individual lives cannot wholesomely exist as island experiences. The community network is vital in ministry.

Clergy composes one of the largest groups of people easily accessible to assist with the care of the people. Other forms of counseling may sometimes not be as assessable or affordable. There are often stigmas, either real or imagined. If for no other reasons than these, it is imperative that clergy be prepared and continue to work most effectively and adequately to provide care for others, both directly and indirectly. Compassion, sincerity, and concern begin the process. (End of passage from submitted paper)

During a Pastoral Care class lecture, we listened to a story about Arthur and the minister who provided Pastoral Care to a man whose quality of life had obviously changed as he neared death. His health was on a steady decline, his home-bound living conditions were unsanitary, and his Pastor became his only visitor. Yet, Arthur, in all of his brokenness, wanted and needed much-deserved dignity. This was honored by his Pastor.

Wherever we are in our lives compared to others or the expectations of others, we deserve respect and dignity. The manner in which we treat those in need buffers the pains and discomforts of our experiences.

This story should have made each of us search our souls, seeking to honestly and clearly identify our levels of commitment to the length of the journeys we are willing to take in the lives of those whom we have accepted the call to serve. We must also recognize our own human limitations and fragility and get the help we need in order to give the help needed. It is imperative to develop the skills necessary to hear, as we seek to be heard. As we go forth to take care of ourselves and our services, we must remain vigilant, devoted, and humble. We must remind ourselves that we are those whom we serve. We all have baggage. We may have dropped off some, but as life goes on, we will pick up more. Pastoral Care and Counseling training can help us to emphatically reach the relevant places in the lives of others as our own personal relevant places are reached.

As Christians and those in leadership, we have a responsibility to help one another through the survival process. Pastor and musician Hezekiah Walker gave us a simple song with an easy melody entitled *I Need You To Survive*. The words of the song begin, "I need you, you need me. We're all a part of God's body...You are important to me; I need you to survive." We may never fully understand one another but we must accept and embrace how important each person is. When we do, it becomes easier to share our gifts, blessings, talents and to unify for the survival and betterment of all.

No matter how good we are, our appearance, our efforts to do everything the best we know how, or how much we have achieved, we all at some point find ourselves in unimaginable life crises that we could never have prepared for. The support, prayers, and compassion of others who embrace us with Godly spirits will help us stay afloat even when we feel as if we are situationally drowning.

"All the people want to know is that you care about them" are the words of a friend and colleague in ministry who has pastored small, primarily geriatric congregations for nearly two decades. Though our lives position us with different requirements and levels of dependency, we cannot live totally without some assistance. Knowing that someone genuinely cares can provide a sense of comfort that helps us feel significant.

Recently I was in conversation with a young minister who began his journey in ministry as a college student with a Bible Study group. He completed seminary and progressed to earn a Doctor of Ministry degree. When we talked, he was leading an older, established congregation of about two hundred people. Many of the families have worshiped at this church for generations. We glossed over what each of us had done since we'd last seen each other. We both enjoyed writing and engaged in conversation about what we were writing. I shared that I was writing about my interest and concerns for congregational care as well as my beliefs that we have a responsibility to provide increasingly more services to help our people to be whole and spiritually healthy. Paraphrasing his words, he said that our people, (meaning African Americans) want a good message on Sunday mornings and want you to visit them when they are sick. "That's it" he said. He politely but harshly disagreed with me that the church and ministers who lead congregations need to do more. I just happened to have been talking to a minister who was verbal and honest about his beliefs. Sadly, many ministers and leaders think the same way he does, and "That's it." Is that really it? Pastor, Do You Care?

It was June of 2011 when the journey for the three of us began in three different cities. Our planes landed at the same major airport within an hour of each other. The organized event we were attending was a Family Unity Conference. Each of us received directions and waited at the designated place for the van service that would take us to our conference destination outside of Boston.

The two of them seemed not to notice my presence, but that was okay. They were neither polite nor friendly. I grew up in the city where one of the men had been the Pastor of a Baptist church for more than twenty-five years. I had even visited the church a few times.

Our driver arrived and put our luggage in the rear of the van. During our thirty-minute transport, I sat quietly on the third-row van seat behind them and looked at a magazine. However, I soon found myself intensely listening to the conversation of the other two ministers as I tried to appear buried in the pages.

Though meeting for the first time, they were clearly not strangers; at least not in spirit. They appeared to have formed an instant bond. Perhaps it was because they had so much in common. They shared that they each served active congregations of about three hundred. Their conversation bounced back and forth like ping-pong balls as they agreed with each other and added lines about their experiences.

One of them told a story about a teenage girl who grew up in the church and her apparent need to share her good news with him. She told her Pastor that she was so excited to be selected as an athletic leader because she had been turned down several times before. "This would have been my last opportunity," she told him. "The problem is I could care less," said her Pastor to the other minister. "Besides, it was Sunday, I had preached and gone to my office afterward. She came and knocked on my door with that mess. Man, I don't care! My time is more valuable than that. I didn't need to hear it and had a hard time pretending that it was good news."

The conversation continued, with one of them admitting that he was being coached by one of his deacons to become more social. He shared that during a recent church fellowship, he stayed in his office while everyone else gathered in the fellowship hall. The deacon called him and highly suggested that he come and join the festivities. He said he agreed to join them, not because he wanted to or cared about what was going on, but because he had an obligation to his deacon and agreed to coaching. Once there, he said that he found a seat in a remote spot where he hoped the people would get the message to not bother him. Then he got a text from the coaching deacon that advised him to move about and interact with the people. "Be friendly" was the message. "Man, I didn't have nothing to say…nothing. Be friendly, he told me. They were not my friends. They were my members." Imagine having to tell the Pastor to be friendly.

The other minister said, "After I preach on Sunday, I'm through with the people. I just want to go into my office and be left alone. I don't want people coming up to me talking about the sermon. I know if it was good or not. I wrote it and I delivered it." *How arrogant can you* be, I thought.

Steering out the window and seeing new sights was as good as it could get on this ride. I found myself unable to be objective or make excuses for either of these two men. I thought *the two of you are so wrapped up in yourself, you should be mummies.* We reached the conference center where, for the next two days a group of about forty ministers would explore and discuss family unity. I had no further interaction with the two of them. Sadly, they are far from being the only ones in ministry who think as they do.

Those who gather in households of faith are families. Unity should begin with the guidance, behaviors, and attitudes of the leaders. Shepherds are to care for their sheep. Spiritual leaders are the people God places in charge. Clearly, there are pains and frustrations associated with ministry. While we know that none of us are exempt from the situations of life; we are also not exempt from showing compassion.

At one church where I served, following most services, the ministers stood near the door of the church. Many of the people would wait in line to share a greeting, a hug, or a conversation. I more deeply realized the importance of these personal moments for the people. "All the people want to know is that you care about them."

As an Assistant Minister and Congregational Care Pastor at First Calvary Baptist Church of Winston-Salem N.C., on most Sunday mornings following Sunday School and prior to the start of morning service, I would go into the sanctuary to personally greet many of the members of this mostly generic congregation. This was a good time to reach out to them. "How are you feeling?" opened the door to many responses. Many of them sat and waited eagerly, sometimes with a hiss or a wave of a handkerchief to get my attention. They wanted the opportunity to share. If they had a matter that I knew about, I briefly mentioned it. Sometimes it was as simple as asking them about an adult child who lived out of town or a grandchild in school. We were very prompt starting our morning worship. Usually, someone would wave or call to me, saying, "You didn't come and talk with me, Rev. Allen." In haste, I would get to one or two more people. In the beginning, I had no idea how important these short Sunday interactions were. It continues to amaze me how much the personal attention of a minister means to some people who faithfully occupy a seat in the pews. Everybody has the need for attention and deserves it. This kind of attention was possible because we had three or four ministers present and a Pastor who saw the value in this kind of interaction.

As a minister in the Supervised Ministry, I was given the opportunity to do some things at this church that hadn't been done before. Rev. Calvin Runnels was my Pastor and supervisor. This required his frequent interaction and meetings with my Supervised Ministry professor. The Pastor listened to my ideas and granted me permission to interact with the congregation in some new ways. We would discuss the outcomes in our one-on-one bi-weekly meetings.

I spent six years at that church, and for nearly three years, I was blessed and privileged to be in ministry full-time. I believe that God prepares each of us to fulfill given assignments. I came to this congregation that was being led by a Pastor who was a Chaplain Supervisor at Wake Forest Baptist Hospital and who had the heart of a chaplain. I was supported, blessed, and privileged to do what my heart led me to do, what life had trained me for and what I believed God expected.

I think I will always recall the bright Sunday morning when we all first met a young man we will call Jordan. As I got out of my car, trying to handle more things than I had arms for, I saw him walking slowly toward me. There was no one else around, and though he appeared non-threatening, honestly, I felt a tinge of fear. I admit, I prayed for my safety as he approached. As we began to talk, I relaxed. He was very polite and began the conversation by saying, "Good morning, Ma'am. Are you a preacher here?" I responded, "Good morning. Yes, I am". He offered to help me with my packages and then said, "I'm not exactly sure what, but I am looking for something." He went on to share that he had been brought up as a Jehovah's Witness but felt a need for something else. He was pleasant and seemed sincere, but there was an obvious emptiness. "Feel your way through and decide if what you are looking for is here," I said to him.

Sunday School had already started, so I invited Jordan to sit in the office with me. Any fear I had was gone. When it was time for service, he went into the sanctuary and found a place right near the front. He was not shy. Without hesitation, he stood up and introduced himself when the invitation was extended. The people warmly welcomed him on that Sunday. He found acceptance and a part of what he was looking for.

The young man continued to come to the church, and a few weeks later, he officially joined the congregation and asked to be baptized. He was excited about coming to Bible Study and shared that he felt a strong need to seek God, unlike he had at other times in his life. He said that it was important for him to share what he was learning with others even though what he had been taught previously was quite different. His words were, "I'm anxious to learn." He'd told me this at our first meeting, and now he is comfortable telling others. He was 28 years old.

The senior ladies loved him because he was young, handsome, and a gentleman. He helped them up and down the steps and carried their packages. The older men loved him because he had the muscles and strength they once had and didn't mind using them. With warmth and a smile, he assisted everyone he could. He didn't mind the dirty work. He carried out the large heavy bags of trash after meals and mopped the kitchen floors. He smiled and was always pleasant. He was easy to love and never a stranger beyond those few tense minutes for me in the parking lot.

Jordan shared portions of his shipwrecked life with us and thanked us at every opportunity for rescuing him. Through several challenging situations, we stood by him and with him until he suddenly stopped coming. Attempts to find him failed. We feared he was facing another gigantic storm. We prayed that he would feel the love of God and that God would be merciful and rescue him again. Much time passed, and I was no longer at that church. A thoughtful member called me with the news that Jordan had returned. "I knew you would want to know," she said. She was right. Jordan called me and thanked me for having been a part of his journey.

I once heard a minister say, "All I want to do is come here, sing my song, preach, and leave. I don't care about anything else." The response to me in reference to the statement was, "That is a preacher who should only have a radio broadcast." A caring minister in leadership stands before the people in the pulpit, speaks messages of inspiration and hope, and stands with the people in times of need inside and outside of the church. People are important. Without them, the church, for what should be its intended purpose, cannot exist. We all have emotional and physical wobbles making it difficult to stand alone. However, I have discovered that when we stand with others, God always has someone to be there for us.

In just a few short years God gave me more opportunities than I could fulfill to demonstrate His love and concern. I visited the sick in their homes, hospitals, hospices, and prisons. I often visited family members who did not belong to the church, knowing that when those we love are hurting, we all hurt.

I cooked in the church kitchen and served in the dining room. I've shared with bereaved families, helped make funeral arrangements, and wrote programs. I've gone to doctor visits and to attorneys with members. The place that caused me the most anxiety was correctional facilities. I visited because it was the thing to do. I wrote letters knowing that those incarcerated needed to be encouraged. Still, there was so much to do and so much to learn. My small contributions seemed so minor in comparison to all that was needed.

Cancer is the savage invader of our physical, mental, and emotional well-being. It not only hurts and destroys the stricken person but also families that often feel helpless in all of their efforts. There are no exemptions from the assaults of cancer. Positions, age, gender, financial status, and education are all irrelevant to who gets cancer. How much we love the Lord and how much of our service we give does not stop the growth of abnormal cells. Among all of the others, three of the closest people to me in ministry have died from cancer: my mentor and Pastor Rev. Calvin Runnels, my friend who served as an AME Pastor for 32 years, Rev. Barbara J. Barbour and most recently my closest and best friend ever, Elder Edna Springs Coleman.

One of the members who grew up in the church where I was serving at the time was challenged in her battle with cancer. We will call her Cheryl. As her condition forced her to be almost homebound, she looked forward to my visits several times a week. She would often be sitting in a chair near the door and, upon my arrival, would laugh and say, "About time you got here." Her son, a young recent college graduate lived with his mother and devoted himself to her care. On this particular afternoon, he eagerly met me at the door. With so much anxiety and concern in his voice, he said, "My mother is lying on the floor in the kitchen. I keep wanting to help her up and she won't let me. Please talk to her Reverend. I think she will listen to you."

I stood for a moment, unsure of what to say or do. This was a first for me. I went into the kitchen where she was lying, stood near, and called her name. "You should get up," I said. The silence lingered, and then she responded, "Why? I'm alright where I am. Why don't you get down here with me?" I hesitated for a minute, then gave the two-letter response, "OK." I got down on the floor and lay close to her. She reached for my hand. We peacefully held hands in long silence. Then she spoke and I listened. Cheryl didn't want responses that day. Mostly she wanted my presence and a listening ear. Finally, she said, "We need to get up from here." My response was, "That's a good idea." I called out to her son who came and helped both of us up from the floor. It was in this most humbling experience, that I learned that there are times when you have to get down with those who are down so that they can get up.

I read about a lady who went to her pastor and told him that God had called her into the ministry. She asked what she should do next. His response was "The bathrooms need cleaning. If you can do that well and not complain than you can be a humble enough person to serve the people of God." I believe many of us could benefit from a good dose of servitude and humility.

# CONGREGATIONAL CARE

T There are numerous biblical passages that clearly tell us how we should treat one another. The Gospels of Matthew and Mark tell us that we should love our neighbor as we love ourselves. The question becomes, how much do we love ourselves? The Gospel of John 13:34-35 (KJV) says, "34 A new commandment I give unto you, That ye love one another; as I have loved you, that ye also love one another. 35 By this shall all men know that ye are my disciples if ye have love one to another." These words remind us that in our demonstrations of love we show others and the world that we are Christians. When we care for one another in the church, those who are not in fellowship see our actions, not as showoffs but as representatives of the God we say we believe in, love and serve. Matthew 20:26 tells us that our greatness lies in our service.

A story circulated throughout the media around 2014 about a church in Ottawa, Canada. Apparently, the church closed its food bank because it attracted too many poor people. The church offered drinks and snacks. But, it decided to stop because the deluge of street people made some church leaders and members uncomfortable. "Most clients of food banks have not yet come to a sense of personal responsibility in life," read one statement about the matter. "They are still in denial, seeing the world as owing them," wrote the pastor of the church. I see this story as a parable about a crisis of care within and emanating from many churches. Christ gave unselfishly to heal the least of us. When we foster true congregational care, we walk in the footsteps of Jesus.

Providing Congregational Care to the church community depends on the needs of the people, the vision of pastors and leaders, and the willingness of the members to make programs work. If the Pastor thinks it is important enough to care for the congregation, then he or she will be instrumental in the development of resources to do so. No person has the mind or ability to do everything, including the Pastor. That is not a negative reflection; rather, it is an intelligent admission to seek assistance for the good. Caring for the congregations requires more attention than the church secretary and the deacons can give. There are qualified people in ministry with the heart, know-how, and training to be Congregational Care ministers. These positions can enhance the respect of the members for the Sr. Pastor and the works of the church. When congregations see and experience the benefits of religious leaders combining their talents for the good of the congregations, everyone benefits.

It is unreasonable to think or expect that any one pastor or congregational leader can do everything when it comes to caring for the people that they serve. However, pastors and leaders must be mindful of needs and be responsible for teaching members the importance of caring for one another. Pastors must first demonstrate non-selfishness and teach the same principles. There should also be a resource bank in the church that refers people to places in the community that can meet specific needs.

The position of Pastor is often the second vocation of many bi-vocational pastors. Combined with many other obligations, effectively caring for the people they are responsible for can be challenging. A Pastor with whom I served said to me, "Rev. Allen, I can't do all of the things you think I should." Setting priorities is important. The wise use of time is imperative. It becomes increasingly important to respect the talents and gifts of others who are available to positively contribute to the holistic approach to ministry that includes caring for the people of God.

The ministry of caring for one another in many churches has long existed with little or no thought of structured programs. People simply looked out for one another, often sharing what little they had. I am reminded of my grandmother and her best friend, who lived just a few doors apart. They had a lifelong friendship, three children each, and very limited assets. Whoever had the meat made a lot of gravy to share, and the other one made biscuits for both families. Especially during the cold and winter season, I know church members who make large pots of soup and share it with people in the church and community. A little of this and a little of that goes into the pot, and it becomes much. There are churches that have soup kitchens that coordinate with other churches in the community to serve on alternate days. Community people in need know the schedules. Feelings of hope come in knowing where and when there will be a meal. Many churches have Blessing Boxes. The box is placed near the sidewalk. There are no locks on the box. Those in need can get items from the box, and those who can give them can put items in the box. It is anonymous.

The history of Soup Kitchens goes back to the 18th century. They show the need for help and the hearts of those who give comfort. With all that has evolved, there continues to be a need for resources to help feed the people of God. Economic crises and pandemics have caused many to seek unexpected assistance to put food on the table and help nourish hungry people, but food insecurities continue.

In one small community that I've been a part of, the church members planted a garden. Some prepared the land; some purchased plants and supplies, and some cared for and harvested the bounty. All that the deer did not eat was placed on a table for everyone and shared. The Pastor, who knew the most about gardening, joyously led and worked with the project.

In the same community at another church, there was a man affectionately called the Vegetable Man. He is retired and has physical disabilities. In spite of whatever obstacles he faced, his mind, heart, and body gave him strength enough to care for so many others. When you saw the little old black truck in the church parking lot, you knew that there was something waiting under the canvas cover for everyone who wanted it. There would be an announcement that the Vegetable Man had potatoes, onions, squash, or whatever fruits and vegetables to share. There were places in lower-income neighborhoods where he parked his truck and called people to come get whatever he had. He shared that the first thing many of them ask is, "How much?" With joy in his voice for the opportunity to be a blessing, he'd say, "It's free! It's free!" At personal expense, he often drove great distances to get the bounty that the farmers gave him. The Vegetable Man was dedicated to his Vegetable Ministry.

The community had a Bread Man. His truck was red. He had arrangements to pick bread and pastries nearing sale expiration dates from area supermarkets. The baked items were put on tables in the basement of his church. Following Sunday service, everyone was welcome to take whatever they wanted. Then he parked the truck outside his home. People walk up to the truck as well as drive up. You helped yourself to whatever is there. He even provided bags. People often ask if they could take an item. "You're not taking." He'd say, "Receive it." While these may seem to be small gestures, it is when we combine our little parts that it becomes a beneficial whole. Like with the fish and the loaves, little becomes much. The community was blessed.

We are serving the same God, so we say. Churches can be built next door to one another or be a part of the same denominational group and too often refuse to work together for the common good of caring for the people. It is unreasonable to expect that any one church can do it all. Congregations in unity can successfully develop and execute beneficial programs. Regardless of religious denomination, we all have basic needs that go beyond the church clothes closet and the once-a-year Thanksgiving basket. We should come together as children of God who demonstrate concern and humility for one another and concentrate on our similarities rather than our differences. Everyone can benefit. This should especially be a consideration for small membership churches and groups with limited resources.

The list of possibilities for care ministries is as extensive as the needs of the people who can be served. Minimal research unfolds many different programs that can be tailored to the needs of particular congregations and communities. Housing programs require planning and significant funding. However, many churches continue to be successful at providing these programs and have done so for many years. Food, clothing, home visits, rides, and prison ministries are among the most popular ministries. Mental Health programs, diabetes, and cancer support groups for those with cancer and their loved ones are important. There are support programs for expectant and new parents, divorce care for adults and children, college and career programs, Grandparents as Parents Programs, Foster Parent Programs, and Military Family Support Programs. There are programs that make pillows, quilts, and prayer shawls for those who need comfort. Bereavement ministries are very important. Millions died from the Covid 19 virus, and millions more still mourn. Again, ministries are as many and varied as the needs of the people.

There are many available resources to assist churches in providing congregational Care. State and County Health Departments and Social Services have established programs and will, in many cases, provide information and personal help to meet the needs of church participants and communities. Some programs only require a referral from the church.

A retired social worker and continued community activist suggested that selected members from small churches in communities come together to create resource booklets of services to benefit members. This would help them to know what services are available and how to access them. Volunteers would do the research, collect the information, familiarize themselves with community services, and speak to the members of the congregations to help point them in the right direction. Collectively the churches would pay for printing and compensate the volunteers for travel expenses. This project would not only provide a much-needed and beneficial guide but would be a demonstration of Christian unity.

There are people who require services but do not come forth because they are embarrassed and have not been given the respect of privacy. Ministries must be carried forth with the highest respect and regard for the privacy and dignity of those in need of care. We must be mindful of unjust suffering in the church and take steps to bring healing and positive change.

**Closing Thought**

Recently I read that sheep are much smarter than they have been given credit for. They supposedly have feelings and especially feel sad when other sheep are slaughtered. As sheep in His pasture, we must meaningfully and mercifully demonstrate our concern for one another. Life situations can slaughter our hopes, aspirations, and dreams. We must work toward providing the much-needed care for the people of God that invigorates and helps all of us as we move toward wholesome and abundant living and service to God.

## CHAPTER X

# "So, Let's Do It"

*"So let's do it—full of belief, confident that we're presentable inside and out. Let's keep a firm grip on the promises that keep us going. He always keeps his word. Let's see how inventive we can be in encouraging love and helping out, not avoiding worshiping together as some do but spurring each other on, especially as we see the big Day approaching."*
(Hebrews 10:24-25 The Message Bible)

As professing Christians, we have an obligation to be representatives of the God we serve. We must put forth our best in carrying out the precepts of Christianity. What better place to start than in the church? Be that bright light, an example for the world to see.

"A church that does not exist to reclaim heathenism, to fight evil, to destroy error, to put down falsehood, a church that does not exist to take the side of the poor, to denounce injustice and to hold up righteousness, is a church that has no right to be... ... I believe that one reason why the church of God at this present moment has so little influence over the world is because the world has so much influence over the church." (Charles Spurgeon 1834-1892)

The church is the major institution designed to guide and develop our lives in the image of God. Worldly influence over the church is not new. However, the beginning of change is within each of us. There must be teaching, conversation, facing harsh realities and truths, and the desire to make a positive difference. Change begins with being open to listening, thinking new and different thoughts, and a change of heart. I've heard it said that we should take our eyes off the behaviors of the people in the church and keep our eyes on Christ. That requires all of us to look in the right places and be good followers. We do not need another excuse to avoid taking honest and objective looks at our behaviors as we accept responsibility and the challenge to work toward becoming our best. We see God through the hearts of our fellow man. We demonstrate our love for God through earthly actions and how we treat one another. God doesn't need anything directly from us. He is God. We all bear the responsibility to show the love of God through our behaviors.

In the 90's, we repeatedly saw the letters WWJD an abbreviation for *What Would Jesus Do*. We cannot do what Jesus was given the power to do by His Father. We can, however, live our lives as representatives of God with Christ-like behaviors. We should live with sincere concern for one another, knowing that we, too, have been blessed with gifts and resources to be a blessing. Our compassion and concern must go beyond our limited little circles. Life should be about more than me, my four, and no more. In our human imperfections, it's alright to self-examine our hearts, attitudes, and thoughts as we seek the word of God for refreshing and renewing. Psalm 51:10 "Create in me a clean heart, O God; and renew a right spirit within me." In honesty, the daily ordeals of life will sometimes overwhelm us and seem to shatter our very beings. God knows that our hearts need healing and restoring daily.

## "SO, LET'S DO IT"

"If a man says, I have love for God, and has hate for his brother, his words are false: for how is the man who has no love for his brother whom he has seen, able to have love for God whom he has not seen?" 1 John 4:20 (BBE Bible Basic English)

If we really want to bring the church closer to the right and bring about change, we must start with a change in heart, love, prayer, Godly leadership, and honesty.

Prayer must be more than a raspy recitation to impress the hearers. Rather, we must all pray and ask God to give us hearts and minds to be leaders and servants as we represent ourselves in the image of God. We must pray for the strength to do the will of God. We must let go of selfish mindsets that have us believing that because of who we think we are and whatever we have been blessed to achieve, grants us permission to conduct the business of God our way instead of God's way.

For some of us, the church is the only place we feel we can be somebody. Be that somebody with Christian integrity. I worshiped with a Sister for several years. She sometimes reminded us that the only place you could continue to go to, act a fool and still be accepted, is in church. Any other organization would revoke your membership had you behaved as some people do in the church. We must stop hiding behind the excuse that none of us are perfect. Of course, we are not perfect but this should not be the permission we give ourselves to act in any kind of way. While it may not be easy, we must work toward being our best for the glory of God.

## The Pastor

Pastors and ministers of the church are to be leaders, guides and example representatives of God and the church. The position of Pastor deserves respect that is earned for more than the title. Esteem should come with service that demonstrates Godly principles and respect for the people God has placed us to attend. There are pastors who say that they run their churches the way God tells them to. Prayerfully, in their hearts, they know that it is God's church, and hopefully, they are listening to the right God. The gods of money and materialism, and the gods of power, control, and dictatorship, will hopefully be silenced in the ears, minds, and hearts of our spiritual leaders. These things have their place, but church is not that place. Money is clearly an important necessity for the success of the ministry, and a workman is worth his or her hire according to the word of God. I believe that when you teach from the Bible and treat people with dignity and respect, people will freely give, especially when there is honesty and openness about how money is used.

In the pulpit and the pew, there must be clarity in knowing and respecting our purpose. We must all come to know better and do better. Our hearts, consciousness, and Biblical teachings must guide us in doing what is right. We must admit that there are problems and trust God in reaching solutions. Those of us in ministry are imperfect. However, using the excuse of imperfection for bad behavior is inexcusable. None of us are immune to consequences. Imperfect leaders can, however, be great leaders when they are compassionate and committed to the calling of God.

The authority of any position in the church should not be abusive. Leadership has a responsibility to learn as well as teach with great expectations of acceptable behaviors. Anything goes should not be accepted in the church. In my efforts to make a difference in a church situation, a minister said to me "These people will not change. Who do you think you are?" I am saddened by those of us in ministry who have such low expectations of the people God has assigned us to serve and resolve ourselves to complacency. People are not like leopards, said to be unable to change their spots or old dogs who can't be taught new tricks. Unlike any other creature made by God, Genesis 1:26 tells us that man is made in the image of God.

**New Members**

Do we want our churches to be exclusive clubs for the selected few, or are we open to others joining us? We either want new members in our churches, or we don't. There is no gray area. If we are sincere in having others join our church families, we must be receptive and show genuine concern. Their presence must be about more than filling our seats and giving us bragging rights because of the size of our congregations or the increase in offerings. Our objectives should be honest and clear. To continue our bad behaviors and thoughtlessness, will continue the revolving doors of the church.

It is extremely important to have a New Members Ministry. Orientations and classes should be well-planned. Here is where the meaning of membership is taught. This is also an opportunity for new members to meet each other and share as they embark upon this new experience. In these groups, questions can be asked, and explanations are given for the uniqueness of this particular ministry. The expectation of the membership is explained. Some new members may be new to the culture of the church and maybe joining a church for the first time. Others may have been long-time members of other churches or other denominations. Each church is different, especially churches that are nontraditional and non-denominational. Church history, leadership, and ministries of the church are important to be taught in these classes.

Everyone has something unique to offer. Sadly, people sit in pews year after year, wasting untapped potential and talents that would bless the people and the house of God. I've had people tell me that no one in the church or ministry ever asked them how they could contribute.

In these classes, leaders have opportunities to identify the gifts of new members and how they can best be incorporated in the works of the church. Spiritual Gifts Assessments or inventories are easily found online. Some are very simple, and others are more detailed. Review several. Based on the congregation and the goals, a selection can be made. These assessments can be done in groups or individually.

Discipleship must fellow as the church must have resources, programs and teachings that help people to fulfill the Gospel. Investing in the spiritual growth of church members must be continuous.

**Challenge and Change**

We must do more than allow ourselves the occasional guilt trip regarding our behavior. Everyone can do their part to institute change and to make a difference. Each of us can be good and decent people, treating others as we want to be treated. As a group, there must be action plans. "Four steps to achievement: plan purposefully, prepare prayerfully, proceed positively, and pursue persistently." (William A Ward 1893-1959) Someone has to emerge as the voice of reason. Every segment of the congregation must be heard and represented. There must be aspiration and leadership skills to make a difference. Everyone must know that their thoughts, voices, and opinions matter. The souls, presence, and concerns of everyone in the church are important. Changes will not happen all at once, but change must start.

Change comes with challenges. "Some people are kind, polite, and sweet-spirited until you try to sit in their pew." (unknown) Sometimes we just have to learn to move, especially our thoughts. We must be willing to unravel the things that stand in the way of our spiritual growth, plant new seeds, pull out weeds, and fertilize the growth. There must be honest self-examination and objectiveness. Be prepared for expected opposition. Let's do it God's way instead of *we've always done it this way.* Change is not always comfortable and comes with growing pains. We all must take a stand for something. "You've never turned the wrong to right. You've been a coward in the fight." (Charles MacKay) Yes, it takes energy to make a difference. When singing, *I'm A Soldier In the Army of the Lord; we must ask ourselves, what kind of soldiers we are.* Let us not be cowardly soldiers. We must be rejuvenated to move beyond being physically and emotionally so tired that anything is accepted from the institution designed to represent God and help us become our best.

**Women In the Church**

Women have power. In order to be taken seriously and help to bring about much-needed change, the women of the church need to bond in united demonstrations of solidarity. Women must respectfully define their expectations of the church with mindful respect for everyone. The church and the women in the church must all be responsible.

While in seminary, one of my classmates, a United Methodist female minister, and I repeatedly found ourselves challenged with the question that I am rephrasing, "What will it take for the church to recognize, respect, and appreciate women in the pew and on the pulpit?" We agreed and always concluded with, "It would take a revolution!" We said that if just half of the women who attended church in this country would all stay home on a planned Sunday and keep their money, male leadership would start to pay attention. Let this movement gain momentum, and in unity, the women stay home two or three Sundays. Undoubtedly, leaders would begin to listen, and change would begin.

Women in ministry must come together in unity to support the ministry and to embolden one another. Rivalry is out of place. Whatever the denomination, we are serving the same God. Though men have dominated the profession of ministry, without any doubt, the roles that women in ministry play are invaluable. How much would it hurt to meet as a group on occasion to listen, share, advise, and encourage one another? It would send a powerful message.

A few years ago, I attended a life celebration service for the mother of a dear friend in the priesthood. Respectfully, I wore clergy attire- a black suit, shirt, and collar. Following the service, a group of Catholic nuns gathered around me, and each of them told me how pleased they were to know that my denomination had bestowed such rights. My age didn't matter, my race didn't matter, and my denomination was irrelevant to them. It was about women celebrating accomplishments. I had never before or since experienced such a moment.

"What you do speaks so loudly that I cannot hear what you say." — (Ralph Waldo Emerson) The powers that be may not want to listen to us as women. Why should they when many women in ministry devalue their contributions and continue to apparently support many male leaders who do not support them? There are some men in ministry who convince women that allowing them to participate in the functioning and service of the church is a privilege. Women must come to understand their value and worth to the organization of the church. Speaking out against the wrongs of the church is not speaking out against God as so many of us seem to think.

We must evaluate our thinking of the treatment of women in the pulpit and the pew. The church must evaluate its response to violence against women. Marginalizing women in the church must end.

**Kingdom Workers**

Everyone must be a missionary. The mission is to do God's work. Church is our learning and assignment center. This is where we learn the lessons so that we can go beyond the walls and carry out the mission of expanding the flock. With planning, purpose, and guidance, we can all serve to help make a difference in the church and community. Laborers are always needed for the harvest.

**An Honest Look**

Business, as usual in the House of God, is in need of renovation. As Christians, we must seriously consider and plan how to better serve the institution of the church and improve our relationships in the church with the people of God. No group of people or denomination that gathers and considers itself a church is exempt from the need to self-examine, submit to honest critique, and make genuine assessments. Congregations must work on ungodly issues and seek counsel and forgiveness. We must weed out the actions that make our churches hot spots and perverse social gathering places of convenience or platforms with ungodly agendas. The church must examine its objectives. Starting with leadership, everyone should be held accountable.

## The Healing Medicine

"Is there no medicine in Gilead? Are there no doctors there? Why, then, have my people not been healed?" (Jeremiah 8:22 Good News Translation) Church is the Gilead of our day. We gather seeking healing for our hurts and a salve for our suffering. We come searching for the answers to the life issues that plague us. We come with the grief and concerns that often hold us spiritual and emotional hostages. We line the pews as we trust God in our dismay and believe that the others who line the pews will show compassion and share the love of God. We gather in the house of God with everyone else who is there because of the grace of God. Grace is the love and favor of God that none of us have earned or deserve.

Everyone in the church deserves to be respected and considered, as everyone will be affected in one way or another. When we know better, we have a responsibility to do better. Our leaders must be held to high standards, and as congregants, we, too, must be responsible. We have no right to complain when we do not demand the best of ourselves. *Is this the church that God is proud of?* We must honestly ask ourselves, then we must collectively work toward making it that church.

And so, the balm, that healing salve, must come through the hearts and minds of those who consider themselves Christians. It must come from church leadership and the people who gather in the house of God. Bearing in mind and in honesty that with all of our imperfections, we are still here. That in itself should be enough to guide us in our preaching, teaching, thinking, and actions. We are ambassadors for the God who knows everything about us. Yet, He still forgives and loves us. We are responsible for treating each other right, especially in the house of God.

## "SO, LET'S DO IT"

Our church experiences, observations, and outlooks differ, and that's a good thing. One night nearing the end of a Bible Study, I passed out a *thought of the week question* that the group was to respond to at our next meeting. "*What can we do to make our church better?*" A few people wanted to respond immediately, but I suggested that they pray for their responses, give it some thought, and be ready for discussion at our next meeting. The oldest member of the church, a beautiful, polished lady in her nineties, called me to the side as others were leaving. She very seriously spoke, "Rev. Allen, I need to talk with you right now. I can't wait for next week." With sincerity, she said, "I've been here at this church for more than fifty years, and I can't think of one thing wrong with our church." We smiled, warmly hugged and I said, "I'm happy about that my Sister, really happy. Please pray for the rest of us."

"The church exists for nothing else but to draw people into Christ." (C.S. Lewis) Let us defeat the giants of self-centeredness as we demolish our territorial attitudes, embrace the importance of everyone, and make our churches houses of healing, not houses of hurt. We must graciously help one another to move from physical, emotional, and spiritual injuries to the healing of open wounds. Let us share the curative balm. Together let us work toward removing scars. And as we do, all of our lives can be made better as together we move toward healing from **Pew Pain**.

> *"For we are co-workers in God's service;*
> *you are God's field, God's building."*
> (I Corinthians 3:9 NIV)

# REFUGE...
# RENEWAL...
# REDEMPTION...

The church, my place of refuge, a healing station

The church, my safe house, a storm shelter

The church, my filling station

Can I get enough to keep me in motion until…

The church doors open again?

For many of us, the church has been our place of refuge, renewal, and redemption. May it continue to be that safe haven that serves to equip us for what lies beyond its walls…LIFE.

Following is a poem from my book **Coal To Diamonds.** It was written and published in 2002. **After The Benediction** is a glimpse of my emotions beyond the church during very challenging times.

### Jude 1:24-25 KJV

[24] Now unto that is able to keep you from falling, and to present you faultless before the presence of his glory with exceeding joy,

[25] To the only wise God our Savior, be glory and majesty, dominion and power, both now and ever. Amen

# After the Benediction

As the past needs the present and the future flashes before me
Time after time, Sunday after Sunday,
Holding to the moments before, having to let go
No luxury of staying in a safe place
I move, I must
**After the Benediction**

"Now unto Him who is able to keep us… To the only wise God…"
Choirs stop singing
Ushers stop seating
Deacons stop praying
The messages of the ministers have ended
**After the Benediction**

Parents hold children on their way out
Brothers, sisters, hugs, embraces, hands shake
Wishes exchanged
Separate ways, separate lives
Silence outside
Screams of panic inside Help!! Help me please
The church doors close
**After the Benediction**

Emptiness of endings
**Fears of new beginnings**
Struggles within to handle within

Struggles without, surround, struggles, struggles
Confusion

**After the Benediction**

"Now unto Him who is able to keep us from falling,
To the most wise God… most wise God"
Wise God
God
Oh God

"…Him who is able to keep us from falling…"
I am falling, falling
I go home alone
To an empty house, or so it seems

I go home
To my angry husband
He wants me not to come back
My complaining wife;
Work too much, she wants me home
Home, she wants more money
Aging parents need my help
Aches and pains remind me, my youth is gone
The children, well God, maybe they are just children
And the rest seem not to even notice

Tomorrow
Bill collectors will call. Thank God for this day off
Boss will be on my back. Thank God for this day off
All week

Needs of others must be met
Can't seem to meet my own
Enough seems never to be enough
Need more love, more money, more time
Sleep too much, can't sleep
Talk too much, say too little
More respect, fewer regrets
Please, Oh God, Please

And while I think I know, I know nothing for sure, except that…
I need you God. I need you!
So much at this moment
After the Benediction

I need to hear your voice as it speaks to my pain, my confusion
I need to feel your gentle strokes of assurance
My total being needs rest in the palm of your hand
Peace I pray as we come closer…together

"Praise Him all creatures here below"
"…All creatures here below"
"Creatures here below"
Below
Oh God, I am your creature here below
I am down Oh God
Your creature is down below and falling
Grab on to me God
Keep my hand in yours
After the Benediction

## PEW PAIN

Keep me in your sight level
Let me hear your voice
Oh God, hold me in your powerful will
Restore my peace. Restore my joy. Restore my faith
Restore and replenish all that needs to be

Press upon my mind that you Oh God are the vigilant one
Who sees all, all the time
Whoever I am, wherever I may be
When I leave this place
When I need you most
Ignite your presence in my life
After the Benediction


Alexis "AHA" Allen
©2001

# Acknowledgments

All of my steps and achievements are because of God and the people He continues to place on my path. It is impossible for me to name every single person who has been a part of my ministry and life experiences. Some people fit in many places in my life and maybe named more than once. **Pew Pain** was many years in the making, even long before pen was ever put to paper. I appreciate everyone who has been and continues to be a part of my life lessons and experiences.

**I am most grateful for those who listened, read many of my thoughts, engaged, and encouraged the narrative.** Dr. Samuel V. Dansokho, Rev. Stephen Wingate, Jean O. Brown, Paula D. Williams, Keith Bolden, Dr. Trevor Eppeheimer, Rev. Horace Means, Ella Joyce Stewart, Linda H. Moore, Yen-wan Hung, Wade Rouzer, Rev. Dorsay Mitchell, Martin L. Harris, Kathaleen Brown, Sakiko Tanaka.

**To my Sisters and Brothers of the Gospel of various denominations, who have encouraged me and poured into my life, many of whom have allowed me to speak from behind their sacred desk…**

Rev. Dr. John A. Lunn, Rev. Stephen Wingate, Rev. Ronnie Roseboro, Rev. Dr. David Bracket, Rev. Delton Nichols, Rev. Dr. Henry Diggs, Rev. Donnie Little, Rev. Shandia Little, Rev. Andrea Polk, Rev. Larry

Myrick, Rev. Sydney Moore, Rev. James Milton, Rev. Juanita Allen, Rev. Georgett Johnson, Rev. Josephine Meachem, Rev. John Jackson, Rev. Mary Metcalf, Rev Regina Dancey, Rev. Thomas Grinter, Min. Annette Joyner, Rev. Ernest Chambers, Pastor Markita Friend, Bishop Robert Melton, Pastor Debra Ellison, Rev. William Rich, Bishop John Krider, Pastor Norzely Krider, Rev. John Pillsbury, Bishop Joseph Johnson, Rev. Brenda Hooper, Rev. William Turner, Rev. Patricia Turner, Rev. Patricia Diggs, Elder Natricia Bailey

**To First Calvary Baptist Church of Winston-Salem N.C. where I served for six plus years as Congregational Care Pastor and Interim, Thank you. To Jerusalem Baptist Church of East Spencer N.C., Thank you for allowing me to minister and serve.**

**To those in my life who studied and prepared themselves to share their knowledge to help others succeed...**

Professor Mark E. Jensen: Chapter III is dedicated to you. Dr. Reginald Broadnax, Dr. Alice Graham and Dr. Andre Resner, you helped me to expand my thought process for which I can never thank you enough. George P. Bush, Mrs. Myers, Dr. Ruben Jones; educators from elementary, middle and high school who set the stage and encouraged me. Sedonia Merrit. To: Tree Turtle, who insisted that I start rewriting Pew Pain from the beginning when I thought I had a perfect draft, and who sent me a new laptop to help with the process, I am most grateful.

**Every role is important...**

Garland Archie, Barbara Blair, Ola Mae Foster, Laura Kennedy, Marilynn Williams, Kenneth Causer, Kelly Woods, Roni Best Simmons, Glendora Hamlet, ♪Thomasina ♪ , Ken Causer, Gates of Zion Church Family,

## ACKNOWLEDGMENTS

Patricia McCallop, The EVS Staff of Atrium Health Lexington Medical Center.

**We all need a Cheering Squad. These are some of the people who have been most reassuring, waving invisible pom-poms and encouraging me in many ways.**

Brenda Kay Evans, Pamala Runnels, Norvis Fonville, Mary Wood, Colette H. Matthews, Sharon Clyde, Beverly Law, Janice Hayes, Karen Whitener, Kathy James, Mozella Lampkin, Priscilla Parker, Kathy Caldwell, Elizabeth Pennix, Sis. Lillie Robinson, Rev. Zenobia Fennell, Randy Williams, Loretta Y. Hawkins.

**Couples**: Clyde and Belinda Rich, Johnny and Natricia Bailey, Willie and Priscilla Parker, Floyd and Carrie Plymouth, Floyd and Darnella Cook, Ed and Selena Holmes, George and Carolyn Napoleon, Hubert and Adine Ijames, Darryl, and Rose Sechriest.

**To My Children who have been on this journey with me** …Clyde H. Rich and Natricia A Bailey, **I love you bunches.**

 **In Loving Memory**

Rev. Calvin Runnels, Elder Edna Coleman, Bro. Frank O'Donnel, Rev. Maye E. Reddick, Rev. Barbara J. Barbour, Joseph D. Jones, Rev. Dr. Olan p. Moyd, Rev. Dr. Raymond Kelly, Henry J.C. Allen, Dorothy Trusdale, Earline Ingram, Kenneth Kirby, Betty Louise Hutchins, Doris Barr, Mary Jackson, Charlie Brown, Edna Greg, Irene Creek, Beulah Wallace, Peggy Roulzer, Sylvester Suggs, Mae Duckett, Rebecca A Hall, my grandmothers: Hilda Gosnell and Annie Hawlins, my mother: Delores Hawkins, my brother: Gregory Green.

_____ Please write your name here. If I inadvertently did not include your name, please forgive me.

**For the special gift of the pen to sign the book and to the giver, my heart says Thank You.**

# To God be the Glory

## About the Author

Alexis H. Allen believes that the pen, like the chisel, has been a gift from God to help her carve her way through many affecting life situations.

She is a native of Baltimore, Maryland, and now lives in Salisbury, N.C. Alexis is the mother of two children, the grandmother of three grandsons and one granddaughter, and is blessed to still have seven living siblings.

She earned a Bachelor of Science in Management from Coppin State University in Baltimore, Maryland, and a Master of Divinity from Hood Theological Seminary in Salisbury, North Carolina. Alexis is an ordained Baptist Minister and was bestowed The George Clayton Tharrington Memorial Award for "Biblical preaching with evangelistic emphasis, keen imagination, creative homiletics, and extemporaneous style."

Her work experiences include teaching in Baltimore City and North Carolina public School Systems and coordinating programs to improve school attendance and increase student graduation. She has served in the church as Congregational Care Pastor and Interim Pastor and is presently a Chaplain Associate in the Atrium Health System.

Prior to ministry I held too many jobs to list. I had several teaching positions in special education including children and adults. I taught

GED classes and adult highschool. For seven years I coordinated a mentoring project and program to increase the number of High School graduates in the Baltimore Public School System. I worked with the same students the entire time. Our sponsors were the Able Foundation and Goucher College.

**Pew Pain** speaks to obstacles, challenges, confusion, and disheartenment too often experienced in the church. Prayerfully, readers from the pulpit to the rear pews will be encouraged to help those in the House of God and beyond and move from hurting to healing.

www.ingramcontent.com/pod-product-compliance
Lightning Source LLC
Chambersburg PA
CBHW070145080526
44586CB00015B/1854